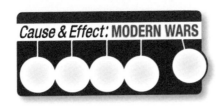

Cause & Effect: MODERN WARS

Cause & Effect:
The Vietnam War

Craig E. Blohm

ReferencePoint
Press®

San Diego, CA

About the Author

Craig E. Blohm has written numerous books and magazine articles for young readers. He and his wife, Desiree, reside in Tinley Park, Illinois.

Picture Credits:

Cover: Associated Press
6: Shutterstock.com/Oleg Golovnev (top)
6: iStockphoto/Peter Hermes Furian (bottom)
7: Shutterstock.com/Marco Rubino (top)
7: iStockphoto/River North Photography (middle)
7: iStockphoto/Sun Chan (bottom)
10: AKG Images
13: Maury Aaseng
17: Vietnam: President Lyndon B. Johnson greets American troops at Saigon, 1966/Pictures from History/Bridgeman Images
20: Vietnam: A U.S. Air Force Boeing B-52 Stratofortress dropping bombs over Vietnam. This aircraft was hit by SA-2 surface-to-air missile over North Vietnam during the 'Linebacker II' offensive on 31 December 1972 and crashed in Laos. The crew of six ejected/Pictures from History/Bridgeman Images
25: Russian Women Go to the Fields, Russia, December 2, 1942 (b/w photo)/Underwood Archives/UIG/Bridgeman Images
30: © Photoshot
33: Ho Chi Minh (1890–1969), founder of Indochinese communist party, then from 1945 president of democratic republic of Vietnam, here on the front c. 1958/Photo © PVDE/Bridgeman Images
37: © World History Archive/Photoshot
41: AKG Images
44: Everett Collection/Newscom
49: Vietnam/Laos: Female communist soldier with AK47 assault rifle somewhere on the 'Ho Chi Minh Trail', 1973/Pictures from History/Bridgeman Images
55: China/USA: Premier Zhou Enlai and President Richard Nixon toast each other, February 1972/Pictures from History/Bridgeman Images
57: Pictures from History/Newscom
61: Vietnam: Refugees from the defeated Republic of Vietnam being evacuated to the flight deck of a US carrier in the South China Sea, April 1975/Pictures from History/Bridgeman Images
65: Shutterstock.com/Everett Historical
69: Associated Press

LIBRARY OF CONGRESS CATALOGING-IN-PUBLICATION DATA

Name: Blohm, Craig E., 1948– author.
Title: Cause & Effect: The Vietnam War/by Craig E. Blohm.
Other titles: Vietnam War
Description: San Diego, CA : ReferencePoint Press, Inc., 2017. | Series: Cause & Effect: Modern Wars series | Includes bibliographical references and index. | Audience: Grade 9 to 12.
Identifiers: LCCN 2016046310 (print) | LCCN 2017005695 (ebook) | ISBN 9781682821688 (hardback) | ISBN 9781682821695 (eBook)
Subjects: LCSH: Vietnam War, 1961-1975.
Classification: LCC DS557.7 .B59 2017 (print) | LCC DS557.7 (ebook) | DDC 959.704/3--dc23
LC record available at https://lccn.loc.gov/2016046310

CONTENTS

"History is a complex study of the many causes that have influenced happenings of the past and the complicated effects of those varied causes."

—William & Mary School of Education,
Center for Gifted Education

Understanding the causes and effects of historical events, including those that occur within the context of war, is rarely simple. The Cold War's Cuban Missile Crisis, for instance, resulted from a complicated—and at times convoluted—series of events set in motion by US, Soviet, and Cuban actions. And that crisis, in turn, shaped interactions between the United States and the former Soviet Union for years to come. Had any of these events not taken place or had they occurred under different circumstances, the effects might have been something else altogether.

The value of analyzing cause and effect in the context of modern wars, therefore, is not necessarily to identify a single cause for a singular event. The real value lies in gaining a greater understanding of history as a whole and being able to recognize the many factors that give shape and direction to historic events. As outlined by the National Center for History in the Schools at the University of California–Los Angeles, these factors include "the importance of the individual in history . . . the influence of ideas, human interests, and beliefs; and . . . the role of chance, the accidental and the irrational."

ReferencePoint's Cause & Effect: Modern Wars series examines wars of the modern age by focusing on specific causes and consequences. For instance, in *Cause & Effect (Modern Wars): The Cold War*, a chapter explores whether the US military buildup in the 1980s helped end the Cold War. And in *Cause & Effect (Modern Wars): The Vietnam War*, one chapter delves into this question: "How Did Fear of Communism Lead to US Intervention in Vietnam?" Every book in the series includes thoughtful discussion of questions like these— supported by facts, examples, and a mix of fully documented primary and secondary source quotes. Each title also includes an overview of the event so that readers have a broad context for understanding the more detailed discussions of specific causes and their effects.

The value of such study is not limited to the classroom; it can also be applied to many areas of contemporary life. The ability to analyze and interpret history's causes and consequences is a form of critical thinking. Critical thinking is crucial in many professions, ranging from law enforcement to science. Critical thinking is also essential for developing an educated citizenry that fully understands the rights and obligations of living in a free society. The ability to sift through and analyze complex processes and events and identify their possible outcomes enables people in that society to make important decisions.

The Cause & Effect: Modern Wars series has two primary goals. One is to help students think more critically about history and develop a true understanding of its complexities. The other is to help build a foundation for those students to become fully participating members of the society in which they live.

IMPORTANT EVENTS OF THE VIETNAM WAR

1955
Ngo Dinh Diem becomes president of the Republic of Vietnam (South Vietnam).

1950
President Harry Truman sends the first US military advisors to Vietnam.

1960
The Communist National Liberation Front (Vietcong) is formed.

1946
The First Indochina War begins as France attempts to restore colonial rule in Vietnam.

1940	1945	1950	1955	1960

1945
Communist revolutionary Ho Chi Minh establishes the Democratic Republic of Vietnam (North Vietnam).

1954
French forces are defeated at Dien Bien Phu, ending hopes for restoring French colonial rule in Vietnam.

1949
Mao Zedong establishes the People's Republic of China.

1964
The Gulf of Tonkin Resolution authorizes President Lyndon Johnson to send troops to Vietnam; Operation Rolling Thunder, the first sustained US bombing campaign against the North Vietnamese, begins.

1965
The first US combat troops arrive in Vietnam.

1969
US troops begin withdrawing from Vietnam; in Paris, secret talks begin between National Security Advisor Henry Kissinger and Vietnamese diplomat Le Duc Tho; US forces begin bombing in Cambodia.

1967
A Gallup opinion poll shows that nearly half of US citizens believe the Vietnam War is a mistake.

1973
The Paris Peace Accords, which halts the fighting in Vietnam, is signed. The last US combat troops leave Vietnam.

1965   1968   1971   1974   1977

1968
The Tet Offensive is repulsed by US and South Vietnamese forces, becoming a turning point in the war. At home, antiwar protests disrupt the Democratic National Convention in Chicago.

1975
The last Americans are evacuated from Saigon as the South Vietnamese capital falls to North Vietnamese forces; Vietnam is united under Communist rule.

1972
President Richard Nixon visits China, marking the start of improved relations between the two nations.

1970
Four students are shot and killed by National Guard troops at an antiwar rally at Kent State University in Ohio.

Fighting for Independence

"We hold these truths to be self-evident, that all men are created equal, that they are endowed by their Creator with certain unalienable rights, that among these are life, liberty, and the pursuit of happiness." When the Declaration of Independence, which contains these stirring words, was signed by the members of Congress on July 4, 1776, the thirteen American colonies were at war with England and its oppressive monarch, King George III. Victorious in the revolution against the Crown, the colonies became the United States of America, guaranteeing its citizens the rights expressed in the declaration. It is human nature to desire the freedom to live life the way one wishes. The type of government under which a society operates either makes that desire possible or makes it impossible to achieve. Thomas Jefferson, author of the Declaration of Independence, further wrote "that to secure these rights, governments are instituted among men, deriving their just powers from the consent of the governed."[1] Many nations have used this assertion as the basis on which to form their own governments. Nearly 170 years after its creation, the Declaration of Independence inspired a revolutionary leader named Ho Chi Minh to declare independence for his country, the Southeast Asian nation of Vietnam.

The Struggle for Freedom

Vietnam had been a colony of France for more than half a century when Ho quoted from the declaration in his 1945 speech proclaiming independence for the Democratic Republic of Vietnam. After restating Jefferson's words, Ho continued, "For these reasons, we, members of the Provisional Government of the Democratic Republic of Viet-Nam, solemnly declare to the world that Viet-Nam has the right to be a free and independent country—and in fact it is so already."[2] By echoing Jefferson's words of freedom and equality, Ho hoped to win the admiration of the United States. But the society he envisioned was vastly different than that of America: It was a society based on the economic and political philosophy known as communism.

Ho's quest to secure independence for his people ultimately led to serious international consequences. After World War II Vietnam was split roughly in half, forming two nations, North and South Vietnam. China and the Soviet Union backed Ho's Communist North, while the United States supported the non-Communist but corrupt regime of Ngo Dinh Diem in the South. The conflict that followed escalated what was essentially a civil war into an international contest between superpowers. The Vietnam War was fought during the post–World War II era known as the Cold War, in which the Soviet Union's domination of Eastern Europe convinced the United States that it was necessary to resist the further expansion of communism throughout the world. When the Soviets developed their own atomic bomb in 1949, the world suddenly had two superpowers, with two diametrically opposed political systems. As a part of the global struggle for dominance between these superpowers, Vietnam became a hot spot in the Cold War. And its impact was felt not only in faraway battlefields, but on the streets of America as well.

"We, members of the Provisional Government of the Democratic Republic of Viet-Nam, solemnly declare to the world that Viet-Nam has the right to be a free and independent country."[2]

—Ho Chi Minh, Communist revolutionary

The American Military in Vietnam

When the first US combat troops entered the Vietnam War in 1965, many Americans viewed US participation in the war as immoral. They asserted that the United States was interfering in another nation's fight for independence, comparing it to America's own revolution nearly two hundred years before. In American cities, violent antiwar protests threatened to tear society apart. On the battlefield, US troops confronted an adversary that seemed to have an endless supply of warriors. No matter how many enemy soldiers were killed, more arrived to take their place. The thick jungles of Vietnam were a refuge where the enemy could regroup after a military loss and return to the

A US infantry regiment conducts a military operation in South Vietnam. Although many Americans opposed US intervention in Vietnam, the majority believed it was necessary to halt the spread of communism in Southeast Asia.

fight even stronger. As the death toll of American troops steadily rose with no end to the fighting in sight, US military and government officials sought a way to disengage from the conflict without damaging America's prestige on the world scene. Ultimately, the United States withdrew from Vietnam—without victory.

Two years after the last US troops returned home in 1973, South Vietnam fell to the Communists, uniting the two nations and ending the war. Vietnam had finally won its freedom from colonial rule and became one nation—united under communism.

CHAPTER ONE

A Brief History of the Vietnam War

For more than two thousand years, the Southeast Asian nation of Vietnam has struggled to retain its independence and secure its place in the world. Bordered on the west by Cambodia and Laos, on the north by China, with an eastern coastline on the South China Sea, Vietnam was ruled by China from 111 BCE to 938 CE. After subsequently enjoying nine hundred years of independence, Vietnam became a French colony in 1887. France lost its colony to Japan in World War II, but in 1946 it sought to restore colonial rule in Vietnam. French intervention was opposed by a Vietnamese independence movement known as the Viet Minh (League for the Independence of Vietnam), led by a Communist revolutionary named Ho Chi Minh. Ho was in control of the Vietnamese countryside and had declared Vietnam to be an independent nation. But France controlled the country's major cities. Armed hostilities between France and the Viet Minh began in December 1946, igniting the First Indochina War (Indochina was the name for the nations on the Southeast Asian peninsula, including the French colonies of Vietnam, Laos, and Cambodia.)

The French War in Vietnam

The First Indochina War was characterized by two different styles of fighting. French military leaders believed that heavy firepower (bombers, tanks, and artillery) would allow their forces to easily defeat the Viet Minh, who were for the most part poorly equipped and poorly trained. The Viet Minh, on the other hand, relied on small bands of guerilla fighters attacking enemy positions and supply depots, then fading back into the dense jungle to regroup and fight another day. Their intimate knowledge of the terrain and the assistance of the local populace in gathering intelligence were a tremendous advantage over the French forces. The Viet Minh greatly outnumbered the French. Thus, despite the imbalances in weaponry, Ho believed he had the advantage and that it would lead to victory. At the beginning of the war, Ho Chi Minh boasted, "You can kill ten of my men for every one I kill of yours. But even at those odds, you will lose and I will win."[3]

> "You can kill ten of my men for every one I kill of yours. But even at those odds, you will lose and I will win."[3]
>
> —Ho Chi Minh, Communist revolutionary

The first years of the war resulted in little progress for either side. French generals were frustrated by their inability to subdue what they considered an inferior enemy. But while the French soldiers were becoming weary of jungle warfare, the Viet Minh were developing into a better-trained and more experienced army. On March 13, 1954, the Viet Minh began a devastating siege of a French outpost in the village of Dien Bien Phu. For nearly two months the besieged French battled to hold on to their isolated garrison, but in the end they were overwhelmed by superior numbers. General Christian de-Castries, French commander of the garrison, radioed his superiors at headquarters, "The Viets are everywhere. The situation is very grave. The combat is confused and goes on all about. I feel the end is approaching, but we will fight to the finish."[4] The finish came on May 7, when the Viet Minh overwhelmed the outpost. Early the next morning, waving a white flag, the French surrendered.

The French defeat at Dien Bien Phu marked the end of France's plan to recolonize Vietnam. In Geneva, Switzerland, a peace conference had begun on April 26, 1954, to decide the fates of two Asian nations: Korea, which had just ended its own war between Communist and capitalist forces, and Vietnam. By July the conference delegates had reached an agreement on Vietnam. Known as the Geneva Accords, the agreement declared an official cease-fire, divided Vietnam roughly in half into northern and southern zones and declared that a general election was to be held in 1956 to unify the two countries under one government. But the election never took place, setting the stage for the Second Indochina War, commonly known in the West as the Vietnam War.

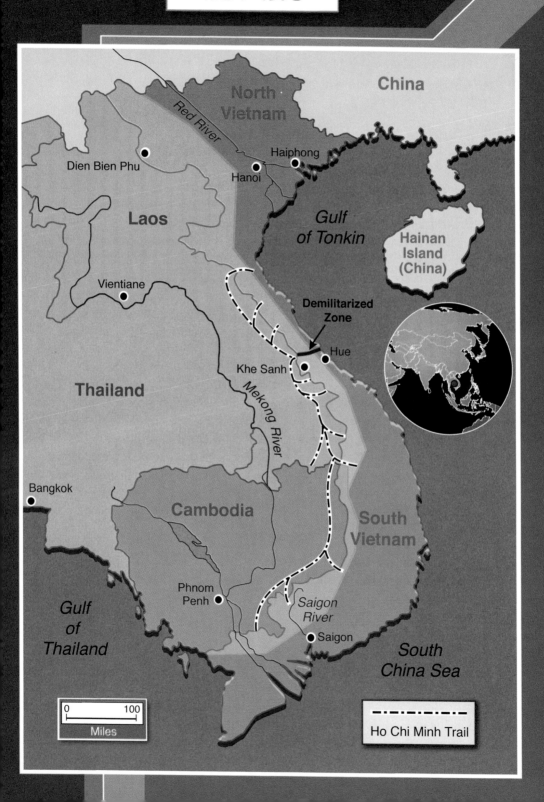

Southeast Asia
1954–1975

China

North Vietnam

Red River

Dien Bien Phu

Haiphong

Hanoi

Laos

Gulf
of Tonkin

Hainan
Island
(China)

Vientiane

Demilitarized
Zone

Hue

Khe Sanh

Thailand

Mekong River

Bangkok

Cambodia

South
Vietnam

Phnom
Penh

Saigon River

Gulf
of
Thailand

Saigon

South
China Sea

0   100
Miles

Ho Chi Minh Trail

Two Vietnams

Vietnam was divided not only by geography but also by ideology. North Vietnam, known officially as the Democratic Republic of Vietnam, had been established by Ho Chi Minh in 1945 as a Communist nation. South Vietnam, known as the Republic of Vietnam, was formed in 1949 by anti-Communist politicians, with chief of state Ngo Dinh Diem ascending to power in 1955. In the struggle to determine the fate of Vietnam, Ho had the support of the Soviet Union and Communist China, while Diem received the backing of the United States.

After the French departed Vietnam, America continued to provide military equipment, advisors, and financial support to South Vietnam's army, known as the Army of the Republic of Vietnam (ARVN). But Presidents Dwight D. Eisenhower and John F. Kennedy both rejected Diem's requests to send ground combat troops to aid the ARVN, which was encountering difficulty in fighting both the North Vietnamese Army, or NVA, and Communist insurgents of the National Liberation Front (called the Vietcong) in South Vietnam. On January 2, 1963, a major battle pitted twenty-five hundred ARVN troops against three hundred Vietcong in the South Vietnamese village of Ap Bac. The vastly outnumbered Vietcong defeated the better-equipped and better-organized ARVN force. It was becoming clear to American politicians and military leaders that without intervention from the United States, South Vietnam would very likely fall under Communist control. But US involvement continued to center on providing advisors and equipment to the South Vietnamese forces.

> "We still seek no wider war."[5]
>
> —US president Lyndon Johnson

America Steps In

That changed on August 2, 1964, when three North Vietnamese torpedo boats attacked the American destroyer USS *Maddox* in the Gulf of Tonkin off North Vietnam. Two days later the *Maddox* and another US destroyer, the USS *Turner Joy*, reported a second attack. These incidents prompted Congress to issue the Gulf of Tonkin Resolution on August 10, which authorized the use of armed US forces in Southeast Asia. President Lyndon Johnson approved Operation Rolling Thunder, the

The Gulf of Tonkin Incident: Fact or Fiction?

The torpedo attacks on US destroyers by North Vietnamese patrol boats on August 2 and 4, 1964, resulted in the Gulf of Tonkin Resolution, which authorized President Lyndon Johnson to begin sending combat troops to Vietnam. But were these attacks real or just a pretext to allow the United States to enter the war?

There was no doubt that the first attack, with the enemy visible on a bright August afternoon, had actually occurred. Two days later Captain John Herrick of the USS *Maddox* reported a second attack to Washington and stated that he had ordered his crews to return fire. This time dark and overcast conditions prevented visual identification of the enemy, so the US ships shot at radar images. But radar is not foolproof when it comes to displaying identifiable targets.

Poor weather and rough seas can create false radar returns that might look like enemy vessels when none are there. The lack of physical evidence, such as damage to the US destroyers or wreckage from sunken enemy ships, created doubts about the second attack. Herrick soon advised Washington, DC, "Review of action makes many reported contacts and torpedoes fired appear doubtful. Freak weather effects in radar and overeager sonarmen may have accounted for many reports." Despite lack of confirmation on this second attack, Congress granted Johnson the power to begin US involvement in the Vietnam War.

Quoted in Daniel Ellsberg, *Secrets: A Memoir of Vietnam and the Pentagon Papers*. New York: Viking, 2002, pp. 9–10.

strategic bombing of North Vietnam designed to disrupt the enemy's ability to wage war by targeting its infrastructure and command capabilities. In a televised speech, Johnson had assured Americans that "we still seek no wider war."[5] But hostilities escalated, and on March 8, 1965, the first American combat troops set foot on South Vietnamese soil.

The first major test of American soldiers, called Operation Starlite, began on August 18, 1965. The operation was a land, sea, and air attack on a Vietcong regiment near a US Marine base at Chu Lai, South Vietnam. After six days of combat, the Vietcong were driven back, suffering more than six hundred casualties to the United States' forty-five. Although Operation Starlite was a decisive US victory, the Vietcong learned how the US used amphibious and airborne attacks to its advantage, and began to develop methods to counter these tactics.

For the next two years, in an ongoing effort to destroy North Vietnamese supply lines and crush the enemy's will to continue fighting, US forces pounded North Vietnam with thousands of tons of high explosives. Neither objective was achieved. Communist forces continued their fight in the jungles and mountains of Vietnam. North Vietnamese fighters died by the thousands, but so did American soldiers. More than half a million American troops were on the ground by the beginning of 1968, a year that saw North Vietnam attempt to end the war with an all-out drive against the South.

Khe Sanh and the Tet Offensive

Along the line that separated North and South Vietnam at the 17th parallel was a 6.2-mile-wide (10-km) strip of land called the Demilitarized Zone (DMZ). The DMZ was a buffer between the two warring nations where military activity was prohibited. To deter the North from breaching the zone, the US established several bases just south of the DMZ, including one built near the village of Khe Sanh, not far from the border with Laos. Intelligence reports indicated that Khe Sanh might come under enemy attack, so the base was fortified with bunkers, trenches, and sandbags. The reports were proved correct on January 21, 1968, when a force of NVA soldiers attacked the isolated outpost with artillery, mortars, and rockets. Within the base, six thousand US Marines repelled the initial assault, but soon some forty thousand NVA troops surrounded the base, settling in for a prolonged siege.

"We are not, repeat not, going to be defeated at Khe Sanh. I will tolerate no talking or even thinking to the contrary."[6]

—General William Westmoreland

There were numerous similarities between Khe Sanh in 1968 and Dien Bien Phu in 1954. Khe Sanh was situated in a valley surrounded by hilly terrain from which the enemy could launch its attacks. Like

President Lyndon Johnson greets troops in Saigon in 1966. After North Vietnamese torpedo boats attacked American warships, Congress issued the Gulf of Tonkin Resolution, which authorized the president to send troops to Vietnam.

the French garrison, Khe Sanh could be resupplied only by air. The commander of the NVA forces at Khe Sanh was General Vo Nguyen Giap, the same officer who had led the siege of Dien Bien Phu. US commanders vowed that Khe Sanh would not see a repeat of the disastrous French defeat. General William Westmoreland, the commander of American forces in Vietnam, emphatically admonished his troops, "We are not, repeat not, going to be defeated at Khe Sanh. I will tolerate no talking or even thinking to the contrary."[6] The defenders at Khe Sanh successfully held off the attackers for seventy-seven days before the Communists finally retreated.

Many historians believe that the Communists used the battle as a diversion to occupy US troops while another, more deadly assault was about to begin. On January 30, 1968, during the Vietnamese Lunar New Year celebration known as Tet, NVA and Vietcong forces launched the largest operation of the war. Abandoning their usual jungle-based

17

In January 1964 a tall officer wearing the three stars of a lieutenant general arrived in Vietnam. William Westmoreland was an old-school soldier who had seen action in World War II and Korea, and he brought his command experience to the jungles of Vietnam. For many, however, his operational strategy did more to prolong the war than to bring it to a conclusion.

As commander of US forces in Vietnam, Westmoreland sought to use America's superior firepower in a war of attrition: to kill more of the enemy than they could replace, destroying their ability to fight. In traditional war such a strategy was effective, but Vietnam was anything but traditional. No matter how many enemy soldiers were killed, there were always more ready to take their place. Westmoreland repeatedly declared that the United States was winning the war. But the 1968 Tet Offensive confirmed that the US was locked in a bloody stalemate with no end in sight.

Westmoreland's tour in Vietnam ended in July 1968 when he was made US Army chief of staff. He retired in 1972 and wrote a memoir entitled *A Soldier Reports*. In 1982 CBS News aired a documentary that accused the general of inflating the enemy body count to create an impression of US progress. Westmoreland sued the network and eventually received an out-of-court settlement. He died in 2005, remembered by some as the general who lost the Vietnam War.

warfare, eighty thousand Communist troops began a massive assault on some one hundred cities and towns throughout South Vietnam. Despite warnings that an attack during Tet was possible, the widespread raids took US forces by surprise. US Foreign Service diplomat Richard Holbrooke noted that Westmoreland was "stunned that the Communists had been able to coordinate so many attacks in such secrecy."[7]

Included among the targets were the ancient imperial city of Hue and the South Vietnamese capital of Saigon. In Saigon the US Embassy compound was attacked, resulting in the deaths of one US Marine and four US Army Military Police before the invaders were repelled. Of the nineteen Vietcong who attacked the embassy, eighteen were killed and one captured. Due to the superior firepower of the US and ARVN forces, most of the Communist attacks throughout South Vietnam were over in a few days. In Hue, where some seventy-five hundred NVA and Vietcong troops had occupied the walled city, fighting continued for nearly a month. When US troops entered the city on February 24, they discovered mass graves that held several thousand bodies of civilians who had been executed by the Communists. The recapture of Hue marked the end of the Tet Offensive.

The Turning Point

The Tet Offensive was a military disaster for the Communists. More than forty-five thousand NVA and Vietcong soldiers had been killed, more than ten times the number of US and ARVN deaths. The operation also failed to accomplish one of its main goals: inciting a general uprising of South Vietnamese citizens against their democratic government. Other than a few isolated incidents, this uprising did not occur.

For the United States, however, Tet marked a turning point in the war. Despite the US victory on the battlefield, Tet proved to American military leaders and politicians that the Vietnam War was far from over. Westmoreland requested 206,000 additional troops to be sent to Vietnam. Back in Washington, DC, Secretary of Defense Clark Clifford warned Johnson that such an increase would result in "more troops, more guns, more planes, more ships . . . and no end in sight."[8] Westmoreland's request was denied. Johnson finally acknowledged that negotiations were the only way to end the war. He called a halt to Operation Rolling Thunder, hoping that ending the bombing would convince North Vietnam to begin negotiating an end to the war.

> "More troops, more guns, more planes, more ships . . . and no end in sight."[8]
>
> —US secretary of defense Clark Clifford

Weary of the stress of war and concerned for his health, Johnson declined to run for reelection. Richard Nixon was elected president in November 1968 and took the oath of office the following January. Nixon had made a campaign promise of ending the war and bringing the troops home, and he began his term in office by withdrawing twenty-five thousand soldiers in the spring of 1969. The following years saw additional troop withdrawals as the ARVN gradually took on more responsibility for fighting the war. But the Communists were not quite ready to give up the fight.

The Easter Offensive

As more US troops were withdrawn from combat, those who remained continued to fight a stubborn enemy. On May 10, 1969, US forces attacked an NVA position in the hills of northwest South Vietnam near the DMZ. For ten days a battle raged as the Communists defended their position rather than escape into the jungle. So fierce was the

A B-52 aircraft drops bombs over North Vietnam in 1972. The US bombing campaign during the Easter Offensive enabled South Vietnam's army to push NVA forces back into North Vietnam.

fighting that it became known as the battle of Hamburger Hill, a name that implied US troops were being sent into a "meat grinder" of death.

At the height of the war in 1968, the United States had more than 543,000 troops on the ground in Vietnam. By March 1972 only 95,000 US troops remained—and only 6,000 of those were combat troops. This left the army of South Vietnam, with 1 million soldiers, responsible for fighting the war. The NVA tested the resolve of the ARVN forces by launching the largest drive into South Vietnam since Tet. Begun on March 30, 1972, the operation was called the Nguyen Hue Campaign by the North Vietnamese; the US referred to it as the Easter Offensive, since March 30 was Easter Sunday. The Easter Offensive was a three-pronged attack, with NVA forces invading South Vietnam across the DMZ and from the neighboring countries of Laos and Cambodia. With 200,000 troops led by Giap and strengthened with artillery and Soviet T-54 tanks, the invading force initially overwhelmed the struggling ARVN forces. Eventually, however, the ARVN regrouped and began making progress against the enemy. What looked at first like a sure victory for the NVA became a resounding defeat when US aircraft began bombing strategic targets in North Vietnam. Called Operation Linebacker, the bombing campaign allowed the ARVN to push the invading force back into North Vietnam.

The uneven nature of the ARVN forces in combat—fighting efficiently in some battles, while being disorganized and poorly led in others—raised concerns about its ability to win against future attacks from the North. It appeared that the only hope of ending the Vietnam War was now in the hands of negotiators who were trying to work out a peace plan in Paris.

An Agreement in Paris

Official peace talks had begun in Paris in May 1968 between the United States and South Vietnam on one side and North Vietnam and its allies in the South on the other. But the negotiations were progressing slowly. Disputes flared over major points such as recognition of a legitimate government in South Vietnam, as well as trivial items like the shape of the negotiating table. The talks continued unproductively for four years. At the same time, behind the scenes Nixon's national security advisor, Henry Kissinger, was conducting secret negotiations with North Vietnamese diplomat Le Duc Tho. These talks ultimately led to the Paris Peace Accords, ratified on January 27, 1973. This agreement called for a cease-fire, the withdrawal of all US troops from Vietnam within sixty days, and the release of all US prisoners of war. The last US combat soldiers left Vietnam on March 29, 1973, ending America's role in the Vietnam War.

For North and South Vietnam, however, the war was not over. The NVA began building up troop strength to mount a final, all-out offensive against South Vietnam, which began in January 1975. Disregarding the provisions of the Paris Peace Accords, NVA forces marched through South Vietnam, conquering city after city as they pushed south. By April the South Vietnamese capital of Saigon was in imminent danger of capture as the enemy approached, shelling the city with artillery and rockets. On April 29 US helicopters evacuated the remaining civilian and military personnel from the besieged American embassy. The next day NVA tanks rolled into Saigon, completing the conquest of South Vietnam and ending the Vietnam War.

The long sought-after unification of Vietnam had been accomplished, and the nation was now under Communist rule. Saigon was renamed Ho Chi Minh City in honor of the revolutionary Communist whose life was dedicated to creating an independent Vietnam.

CHAPTER TWO

How Did Fear of Communism Lead to US Intervention in Vietnam?

Focus Questions

1. What are the benefits and pitfalls of capitalism? What are the benefits and pitfalls of communism? Which system would you rather live under and why?
2. Was containment the best strategy for dealing with communism? If so, how so? If not, what other approach do you think may have yielded better results and why?
3. Was America's fear of communism justified or exaggerated—and in what ways?

On April 3, 1954, eight members of Congress arrived at the US Department of State in Washington, DC, to attend a secret meeting led by Secretary of State John Foster Dulles. As they entered a conference room, the men were met by Dulles, who greeted them with a solemn announcement: "The President has asked me to call this meeting."[9] The presence of several high-ranking military commanders intensified the gravity of the gathering.

The purpose of the meeting was to obtain congressional support for a plan to handle a crisis in the Vietnamese town of Dien Bien Phu. Since March the French garrison there had been besieged by Communist Viet Minh forces, which were daily pummeling the outpost with artillery fire and infantry raids. As the French troops had to rely on increasingly hazardous air drops for food and ammunition, it appeared that the garrison could not hold out much longer.

The Americans had grave concerns about the possibility of a French defeat. US leaders feared that communism would spread throughout Southeast Asia if the Viet Minh were victorious. One worry was that a Communist government in Vietnam might block US access to the country's many natural resources, a move that could hurt US industries that relied on those resources. But the larger worry was the proximity of a Communist country to Japan, America's most important ally in that region and the possibility of communism gaining a foothold in Southeast Asia. Admiral Arthur W. Radford, chair of the Joint Chiefs of Staff, presented his plan to save Dien Bien Phu: massive US air strikes against the Viet Minh forces, launched from bases in the Philippines and from aircraft carriers in the South China Sea. What made this proposal especially chilling was that it included the use of three atomic bombs against the enemy. Doing so would create enormous worldwide political repercussions, and it could destroy not only the enemy but the French outpost as well. The congressmen asked Radford questions concerning the cost of the operation, the likelihood of success, and whether any of America's allies had been consulted. The meeting ended with the congressmen suggesting that the military enlist the aid of allied nations before staging the operation.

The plan, called Operation Vulture, never got off the ground. President Dwight D. Eisenhower was unable to convince any allies, especially Great Britain, to join the operation. The fall of Dien Bien Phu in May 1954 made it clear that the French forces could no longer stem the Viet Minh tide. Eisenhower told British prime minister Winston Churchill that if the rest of Vietnam fell to communism, "the consequent shift would be disastrous."[10] Fear of such a shift would drive the United States into a war it could not win.

Communism and Capitalism

At the heart of America's stake in Vietnam was its policy of preventing communism from spreading throughout the world. Since its birth as a nation, America has operated under the economic and social system known as capitalism. Capitalism is a free-market system in which the means for producing goods rests with the individual. Anyone can create a product and sell it for a profit. Citizens may own property, accumulate personal wealth, create businesses, and hire workers for their factories and stores. In America the government does not control the capitalist system, although it can make laws such as setting a minimum wage that workers must be paid and ensuring the safety of products.

Opposing the concepts of free markets and individual property is the economic and political system known as communism. The theory of communism was developed by German philosopher Karl Marx in the nineteenth century. Under communism, all industrial production is owned and controlled by the government. Every citizen works for the government, and everyone receives what the government decides he or she is entitled to. The Communist creed is, in Marx's words,

Russian farmworkers head to the fields of a collective farm in the 1940s. The Soviet Union was the first nation to be governed by the principles of communism, which opposes free markets and private property.

"From each according to his ability, to each according to his needs!"[11] Marx envisioned a society in which poverty and class distinctions would not exist, collective farms would grow enough food for the masses, and state-run factories would produce steel, iron, and military weapons. To the Communists, such an idealized society would be the solution to all the world's problems. Marx believed that capitalism was doomed to fail and that communism would become the world's leading social and economic system. The Soviet Union was the first nation to be governed according to the principles of communism, and its leaders were determined to spread their philosophy as far and wide as possible, using whatever means necessary.

> "From each according to his ability, to each according to his needs!"[11]
>
> —Karl Marx, nineteenth-century German philosopher

Communism Grips Eastern Europe

The division of Vietnam into Communist and capitalist regions in 1954, and the fact that North Vietnam was backed by powerful Communist China, led to mounting fear that communism would spread from North Vietnam to South Vietnam—and then to other countries. In a letter to South Vietnam's President Diem on October 23, 1954, Eisenhower wrote:

> I have been following with great interest the course of developments in Vietnam, particularly since the conclusion of the conference at Geneva. The implications of the agreement concerning Vietnam have caused grave concern regarding the future of a country temporarily divided by an artificial military grouping, weakened by a long and exhausting war and faced with enemies without and by their subversive collaborators within.[12]

Eisenhower had good reason to fear Communist expansion in Asia. As the supreme commander of Allied forces in Europe during World War II, he saw firsthand how the Soviet Union had moved to dominate Eastern Europe. On February 4, 1945, three months before

The rise of Communist nations became such a troubling development for the United States that an official committee was established to root out Communists who, many feared, had infiltrated American industry and government. The House Un-American Activities Committee was formed in 1938 as a committee of the US House of Representatives. Its mandate was to identify Americans suspected of subversive activities and bring them before Congress for questioning. Government employees were prime targets for the committee's investigations. Hollywood directors, writers, and stars were also high on the list of potential Communists.

Holding public hearings, the committee's interrogation techniques were intimidating to those who were called to refute allegations of Communist ties, against either themselves or acquaintances and coworkers. Failure to provide information or to identify others suspected of being Communists could result in a prison sentence. Just being called to testify often caused job losses and a ruined life—even for those who had no ties to communism. Invoking the Fifth Amendment right against self-incrimination automatically cast a shadow of suspicion from which it was difficult to recover.

By the 1960s the House Un-American Activities Committee had begun to lose its influence, in part due to America's growing distaste for its Communist "witch-hunting." The committee disbanded in 1975, but in the years it was active it was able to convince many Americans that Communists lurked around every corner, ready to destroy their comfortable way of life.

the war in Europe ended, the "Big Three" Allied heads of state met at the Black Sea port city of Yalta in Crimea, then a part of the Soviet Union. US president Franklin D. Roosevelt, British prime minister Winston Churchill, and Soviet premier Joseph Stalin had come together to determine the fate of European nations, especially Poland, in the postwar world.

By the end of the conference, the three leaders agreed that they would help the countries that had been under German occupation during the war establish democratic governments. They also mandated that Poland's provisional government, installed by the Soviets, be subject to free elections within a month. But Stalin reneged on the agreement, and rather than holding an election, Poland remained firmly under Communist influence. After the war ended, other nations of Eastern Europe that had been liberated by the Soviet Red Army—Hungary, Romania, Bulgaria, and Czechoslovakia—were absorbed into the Soviet sphere of influence and remained under Communist control.

In a March 5, 1946, speech, Churchill used an evocative term when describing the influence of communism throughout Eastern Europe:

> From Stettin in the Baltic to Trieste in the Adriatic an "Iron Curtain" has descended across the continent. Behind that line lie all the capitals of the ancient states of Central and Eastern Europe.... All these famous cities and the populations around them lie in what I must call the Soviet sphere, and all are subject, in one form or another, not only to Soviet influence but to a very high and in some cases increasing measure of control from Moscow.... This is certainly not the liberated Europe we sought to build up. Nor is it one which contains the essentials of a permanent peace.[13]

Behind the Iron Curtain, communism ruled. The possibility of further expansionism by the Communists led to an important concept in American foreign policy: containment. In 1947 diplomat George F. Kennan wrote an article in the journal *Foreign Affairs*, stating that "the main element of any United States policy toward the Soviet Union must be that of a long-term, patient but firm and vigilant containment of Russian expansive tendencies."[14] Kennan's recommendation of containing Communist expansion influenced President Harry Truman, and containment became a part of the president's postwar foreign policy, known as the Truman Doctrine. "I believe," Truman told Congress on March 12, 1947, "it must be the policy of the United States to support free peoples who are resisting attempted subjugation by armed minorities or by outside pressures."[15] With the policy of containment, Truman hoped to allay

America's fear of communism spreading further around the world, possibly to the United States itself. But as a new decade dawned, that fear proved difficult to dispel.

The Red Menace

Rising fear of communism permeated American society in the 1950s. After Stalin died in 1953, he was succeeded as premier in 1958 by Nikita Khrushchev, the leader of the Soviet Communist Party. Even before coming into office, Khrushchev made his opinion of capitalism clear. In a 1956 speech, he shouted to Western diplomats, "About the capitalist states, it doesn't depend on you whether or not we exist. . . . Whether you like it or not, history is on our side. We will bury you!"[16] Less than a year later, it seemed that Khrushchev's warning could come true.

On October 4, 1957, Americans woke up to the news that the Soviet Union had launched an artificial satellite named *Sputnik* into Earth's orbit. Many people were afraid that the tiny spacecraft was actually an orbiting bomb. Although that fear was unfounded, the true import of *Sputnik* was clear: If Soviet missiles could launch a satellite into orbit, they could also deliver atomic bombs to any target in the United States. Still lacking such powerful missiles,

> "About the capitalist states, it doesn't depend on you whether or not we exist. . . . Whether you like it or not, history is on our side. We will bury you!"[16]
>
> —Nikita Khrushchev, Soviet premier

the United States was falling behind in the nuclear arms race, and its citizens were increasingly afraid. Weekly tests of air raid sirens rattled the nerves of the average American. Schools held drills in which a nuclear bomb had supposedly exploded, sending students scrambling into corners or under their desks in a maneuver known as "duck and cover." Many Americans built bomb shelters in their basements or backyards as protection from the radioactive fallout produced by an atomic bomb blast. Perhaps the most visible example of the fear of communism in America was demonstrated by Joseph McCarthy, a senator from Wisconsin. McCarthy declared that the US government—including the army—had been infiltrated by Communists. His

A schoolteacher in Chicago leads her students in a "duck and cover" air raid drill in the 1950s. The Soviet Union's growing nuclear capabilities made Americans fearful of an impending nuclear attack.

bullying tactics and outrageous claims made for sensational headlines, but his investigations never produced a single Communist.

Although McCarthy and his claims were ultimately discredited, the affair demonstrated the fear of communism that held the United States in its grip during the 1950s. While the Soviet Union's nuclear capabilities were sowing seeds of fear in America, another Cold War hot spot was developing in Asia.

Korea and China

In the aftermath of World War II, the Asian nation of Korea was divided into two regions, Communist North Korea and democratic South Korea. Each government felt that it was the legitimate regime for all of Korea, and in June 1950 war broke out. Backed by the Soviet Union, North Korean troops invaded the South, driving South Korean forces back to a small perimeter around the southern port city of Pusan. Truman was alarmed by the possibility of this new Communist aggression escalating into a war that could envelop not only Asia but Western Europe as well. This fear grew out of memories of Eastern Europe succumbing to Communist expansion after World War II. He convinced the United Nations (UN) to deploy a military force, led by the United States, to aid South

The Missile Gap

During the 1950s and 1960s, there was nothing more frightening than the thought of the Soviet Union, the world's most powerful Communist country, building a huge arsenal of nuclear weapons to destroy the United States. With the launch of the satellite *Sputnik* in October 1957, the Soviets proved they had missiles powerful enough to carry a nuclear warhead to the United States. In contrast, America was having trouble developing missiles with similar capabilities. US intelligence predicted that by 1965 the Soviet Union would have up to one thousand intercontinental ballistic missiles (ICBMs) aimed at the United States, while the United States would have a mere seventy available to retaliate. Such a large disparity in nuclear capability gave rise to the term *missile gap*, fueling fears that America was vulnerable to a nuclear first strike by the Soviet Union.

Unknown to Americans, however, was the fact that there was no missile gap. When new high-altitude spy planes were flown on photographic intelligence missions over the Soviet Union in the 1960s, they uncovered no evidence of a mass buildup of Soviet ICBMs. They could not find even one ICBM deployed and ready for launch. Early intelligence estimates were faulty, creating the idea of a missile gap that did not in fact exist. Although the missile gap was a myth, it served to heighten the fear of communism in a world that seemed to be edging ever closer to a conflict between opposing ideologies.

Korea. As Truman recalls in his autobiography, "If we had not persuaded the United Nations to back up the free republic of Korea, Western Europe would have gone into the hands of the Communists."[17]

By September, UN troops had pushed the Communist forces back to the Yalu River, the border between North Korea and the People's Republic of China. Often referred to in the West as Red China, the nation was established in 1949 by Communist revolutionary Mao Zedong. Concerned with having UN troops so close to the Chinese border, Communist Party chair Mao prepared his army to enter the war. In response to a UN advance, some three hundred thousand Red Chinese troops poured across the Yalu River on November 25, 1950, pushing UN forces back to the 38th parallel, the line separating North and South Korea. Fighting continued until July 27, 1953, when an armistice was agreed on, bringing hostilities to a halt. But a peace treaty was never negotiated, meaning the war never officially ended. This kept North and South Korea in a perpetual stalemate that could escalate into war at any time.

Korea was the first military clash of communism versus democracy. But it was not the only Asian trouble spot. Some 2,100 miles (3,380 km) to the southwest, Vietnam was becoming a powder keg that would ultimately explode into a long and costly international conflict.

Keeping Communism Out of Vietnam

For years the United States had been following French military operations in Vietnam with growing concern over the lack of progress against the Viet Minh. Beginning in 1948 under Truman, the United States had been supporting the French forces by providing funds and military equipment. Continuing under the Eisenhower administration, US aid to France eventually totaled more than $2.6 billion. It was a staggering sum but was justified in part by economic necessity. Asia held an abundance of raw materials needed for industry in the United States and other free-world nations. After touring Southeast Asia in December 1953, Vice President Richard Nixon explained in a television and radio speech the importance of keeping communism out of Indochina:

> If Indochina falls, Thailand is put in an almost impossible position. The same is true of Malaya with its rubber and tin. The same is true of Indonesia. If this whole part of Southeast Asia

goes under Communist domination or Communist influence, Japan, who trades and must trade with this area in order to exist, must inevitably be oriented toward the Communist regime. That indicates to you and to all of us why it is vitally important that Indochina not go behind the Iron Curtain.[18]

The Tiger and the Elephant

The similarities between Korea and Vietnam are apparent. Each nation was divided in two, and each had strong financial and military support from powerful, politically aligned backers: the Soviet Union and China in the North, and the United States in the South. The northern half of each country shared a border with the powerful, and supportive, Communist China. The dictator of North Korea, Kim Il Sung, and the leader of North Vietnam, Ho Chi Minh, were both fighting to unite their separate countries under Communist rule.

Backed by China and the Soviet Union, Communist revolutionary Ho Chi Minh (foreground) defeated the French at Dien Bien Phu, sparking fear that communism would spread throughout Southeast Asia.

As French troops began their futile struggle to defeat the elusive Viet Minh in the early 1950s, Ho Chi Minh predicted the war would be like a fight between a tiger and an elephant. "If the tiger ever stands still," Ho said, "the elephant will crush him with his mighty tusks. But the tiger will not stand still. He will leap upon the back of the elephant tearing huge chunks from his side, and then he will leap back into the dark jungle. And slowly the elephant will bleed to death. Such will be the war in Indochina."[19]

Ho's prediction became a certainty when China began providing military training and weapons to the Viet Minh. This presented a serious problem for the United States and its policy of containment: If communism took hold in Vietnam, other nations in Southeast Asia could also fall. In a press conference on April 7, 1954, Eisenhower compared the situation to a row of dominoes, where "you knock over the first one, and what will happen to the last one is the certainty that it will go over very quickly. So you could have a beginning of a disintegration that would have the most profound influences."[20] Commonly referred to as the domino theory, it became a key concept in America's Cold War policy. Eisenhower was well aware that Vietnam could become the first domino in Southeast Asia.

> "Nearly all American officials . . . perceived Vietnamese communism as one of the fronts of contest with the Soviet Union and China. . . . Vietnam remained a 'domino' whose fall would undermine and topple noncommunist regimes in neighboring states."[21]
>
> —Historian George Kahin

The fear of communism spreading worldwide was the underlying cause of the Cold War, and Vietnam became that war's most controversial battlefield. As historian George Kahin writes, "Nearly all American officials . . . perceived Vietnamese communism as one of the fronts of contest with the Soviet Union and China. . . . Vietnam remained a 'domino' whose fall would undermine and topple noncommunist regimes in neighboring states."[21]

In 1965 the first of what would eventually grow to a force of more than half a million troops stepped ashore in Vietnam, prepared to prevent the ancient nation from being drawn into the Communist sphere. Half a world away, America was counting on its military might to keep the first domino from toppling.

CHAPTER THREE

How Did the Tet Offensive Increase Opposition to the War?

Focus Questions

1. Why do you think most Americans initially supported US involvement in Vietnam, and why did that change after the Tet Offensive?
2. How did television influence the American public's understanding of the Vietnam War?
3. What part did antiwar protests play in helping bring an end to the Vietnam War?

Tet, the Vietnamese Lunar New Year celebration, is the most important holiday in Vietnam. Occurring in late January or early February, Tet celebrates the coming of spring with fireworks, parades, and family reunions. As the holiday approached in 1968, however, there were ominous hints that something would be different about that year's celebration. On January 1 a poem was broadcast on Radio Hanoi, North Vietnam's government-run station:

> This Spring far outshines the previous Springs,
>
> Of triumphs throughout the land come happy tidings.
>
> Let North and South emulate each other in fighting the U.S. aggressors!
>
> Forward!
>
> Total victory will be ours.[22]

The author of the poem was Ho Chi Minh himself, calling for a united Vietnam to defeat the American troops, a foreshadowing of the offensive to come. The day after the poem was broadcast, US Marines killed five NVA officers who were conducting a reconnaissance patrol near Khe Sanh, another sign that an attack was in the offing. In fact, North Vietnam's planning for a massive attack had been going on since the summer of 1967. In September Radio Hanoi broadcast a message from General Vo Nguyen Giap that could have been interpreted as a blueprint for the upcoming operation. By December US intelligence reported an unusual increase in traffic along the Ho Chi Minh Trail, North Vietnam's covert supply route through the neighboring countries of Laos and Cambodia. The Vietcong were secretly hiding supplies, weapons, and ammunition in strategic areas around South Vietnam.

General William Westmoreland was expecting an enemy offensive to start off the new year. In fact, he seemed to be eagerly anticipating it. "I hope they try something," Westmoreland told a *Time* magazine reporter in November 1967, "because we are looking for a fight."[23] But he badly misjudged the intent of the enemy. When fighting began in Khe Sanh near the DMZ on January 21, Westmoreland was certain that the North Vietnamese would use the village to try to re-create their 1954 victory over the French at Dien Bien Phu. The general told his superiors in Washington that "the enemy will attempt a country-wide show of strength just prior to Tet, with Khe Sanh being the main event."[24] Because of his miscalculation, Westmoreland and his forces were unprepared for the actual main event, which began on January 30, 1968.

The Battle Begins

While South Vietnamese families were busy preparing their holiday celebrations, they were unaware that thousands of NVA and Vietcong troops lay in hiding, waiting for word to spring into action. That command came from Giap with the words, "Crack the Sky, Shake the Earth,"[25] the message that the battle was to begin.

Shortly after midnight on January 30, the first attacks of the offensive targeted several South Vietnamese provincial capitals as a prelude to the main assault. At around three o'clock on January 31, between seventy thousand and eighty thousand Communist troops began a massive, coordinated assault on more than one hundred South

Vietnamese civilians sort through the ruins of their homes in Saigon following the Tet Offensive. During the three weeks of combat in January and February 1968, more than fourteen thousand civilians were killed.

Vietnamese cities and towns, as well as numerous US and ARVN installations. Among the targets were supposedly secure cities such as Da Nang, Qui Nhon, the ancient imperial city of Hue, and the Communists' most important objective, the South Vietnamese capital of Saigon. After years of jungle warfare, US and ARVN troops found that fighting in crowded cities and towns was a grueling way to wage war. "The city of Hue was almost totally in the hands of the enemy," recalls Joseph Galloway, a United Press International reporter following US troops in Vietnam. "It would take about a month or more for the Marines to retake it, and at terrific casualties because they were fighting house-to-house, room-to-room, in a city environment. Urban warfare is really brutal, really vicious, and very costly in terms of casualties."[26]

One of the main objectives of the Tet Offensive was Saigon, where the US Embassy came under attack at 2:30 a.m. on January 31. Nineteen Vietcong insurgents in several trucks roared up to the embassy

Internationally recognized military historian James H. Willbanks was an infantry advisor in Vietnam. Among his books on the war is *The Tet Offensive: A Concise History*, in which he discusses the impact of television coverage of the Tet Offensive.

> The role of the media during the Vietnam War remains controversial, and there has been a long-standing argument that the coverage of the war and particularly the Tet Offensive ultimately led to the American defeat in Vietnam. It is true that as the war progressed, televised coverage of the fighting in Vietnam became more and more important to changing public opinion. Vietnam was the first war covered extensively on U.S. television, and by the time of the commitment of American combat troops in 1965 more than half of the American people relied on TV as their principal source of news.
>
> The media coverage of the Tet Offensive had a great influence on the eventual outcome of the fighting and its aftermath. The reporters did not believe the official statements that came out of the Military Assistance Command, Vietnam (MACV) [responsible for all US forces in Vietnam] during and after the bloody fighting of the offensive, and the media coverage generally reflected this disbelief.

James H. Willbanks, *The Tet Offensive: A Concise History*. New York: Columbia University Press, 2007, p. 110.

compound, which contained several structures, including the newly completed main office building. After blowing a hole through the wall surrounding the compound, the Vietcong insurgents entered the compound and killed five military guards. US Foreign Service officer Allan Wendt, who was inside the main office, recalls that morning. "Suddenly, the building was rocked by a loud explosion. Automatic weapons fire broke out, and rockets began to thud into the building. The embassy was under attack."[27] After failing to gain entry to the offices, the Vietcong dug in and began shooting at marines called in to counter the attack. After a six-hour firefight, the bodies of eighteen of the Vietcong insurgents littered the embassy grounds; the remaining guerilla was captured.

As widespread fighting continued, US and ARVN forces managed to retake control of South Vietnam, inflicting massive casualties on the Communist enemy. The Tet Offensive ended on February 24, 1968, when the last Communists were defeated at Hue. During the three weeks of combat, more than 1,500 US soldiers and marines were killed, along with 2,788 ARVN troops. Communist casualties numbered some 45,000 killed, and more than 14,000 civilians lost their lives. Although the Tet Offensive was a military defeat for the NVA, it was a psychological victory for the Communists: America's opinion of the US mission in Vietnam was about change.

Gauging Public Opinion

Public opinion about Vietnam was difficult to ascertain in the late 1950s and early 1960s. The dangers of the Cold War had entered the American consciousness with the growing nuclear arms race between the United States and the Soviet Union. But few people knew that the United States had been sending military advisors to Vietnam for years or that the conflict was slowly escalating. By the time of the Gulf of Tonkin incident in 1964, people were beginning to take more notice of and voice their support for US involvement in Southeast Asia. In a poll taken by the *Saturday Evening Post* in 1965, 65 percent of those questioned felt that the United States should stay in Vietnam, even if the war meant a prolonged commitment of US soldiers.

But as the war dragged on, the number of people opposed to the war gradually began to rise. According to Gallup, a research company that conducts opinion polls on various topics, in August 1965, 24 percent of Americans considered US involvement in Vietnam a mistake. A month before Tet, another Gallup poll revealed that that number had crept up to 44 percent. Seven months after the Tet Offensive, an August 1968 poll revealed that 53 percent of Americans now saw US involvement in Vietnam as a mistake. It was the first time that a majority of Americans had expressed disapproval of the conduct of the war; this disapproval was reflected mainly by the antiwar activities on America's college campuses.

Protesting the War

As awareness of the Vietnam War increased, college students began to protest against American involvement in the war. One of the earliest strategies used by the antiwar movement was the teach-in. Usually conducted by students and faculty on a college campus, teach-ins used speeches, workshops, films, and discussions as a way to educate people about the war. Sit-ins, in which groups of protesters seize a room or building to deny access to its rightful occupants, cropped up on many college campuses, and mass demonstrations were held in numerous US cities. Young men who were eligible to be drafted for military service often burned their draft cards in protest, defying a federal law banning such action. College student Martin Jezer, who burned his draft card in 1967 despite the fear of jail, recalls, "I had no doubt that this is what I had to do. . . . [I knew that] [s]ome of us [would] have to face imprisonment with joyous defiance."[28]

> "I had no doubt that this is what I had to do. . . . Some of us will have to face imprisonment with joyous defiance."[28]
>
> —Protester Martin Jezer, on burning his draft card

Another protest tactic was the creation of a national moratorium: a day set aside to suspend normal activities and attend teach-ins, peace marches, and prayer vigils. Millions of people all across the country participated in such protest activities, highlighting the public's change in attitude against the war. Although most of these events were peaceful, one notoriously violent demonstration occurred at the August 1968 Democratic National Convention in Chicago.

The news media were out in force as delegates gathered to choose the Democratic candidate for president. Numerous protest groups also converged on Chicago to stage antiwar protests, which soon turned violent. As thousands of mostly youthful demonstrators filled the streets of downtown Chicago, they were confronted by more than eleven thousand Chicago police officers in riot gear. Under orders from Mayor Richard J. Daley, the police used nightsticks and pepper spray to subdue the protesters. Television camera operators and still photographers, many of whom were also attacked by police, kept filming as officers beat and arrested hundreds of demonstrators while the protesters chanted, "The whole world is watching! The whole world is watching!"[29]

Protesters hold a sit-in in front of the Pentagon in 1967 as military police block the entrance. As public support for the war waned, millions of people attended antiwar demonstrations throughout the United States.

Millions of people were indeed watching as the scenes of police brutality flashed from the streets of Chicago to living rooms across the nation and around the world. Television was demonstrating the power of visual media to change minds and opinions.

Tet and Television

Since the first US combat troops entered the war in 1965, television news coverage consisted mostly of positive reports of American troops engaging the enemy and emerging victorious after each battle. In broadcasting nightly statistics on enemy soldiers killed, known as the body count, TV reinforced the military's assertion that the United States was winning the war. Editorial commentary concerning President Lyndon Johnson's handling of the war was favorable by a margin of four to one.

The Kent State Shooting

Of the many antiwar protests staged during the Vietnam War, none was more tragic than what happened on a warm May afternoon in 1970 on the campus of Kent State University in Kent, Ohio. For three days beginning on May 1, student protesters had demonstrated on campus to protest President Richard Nixon's expansion of the war into Cambodia. After some students set about vandalizing businesses in downtown Kent, Governor James Rhodes called out the Ohio National Guard to help police control the situation. Another campus rally began on May 4, even though it was banned by university authorities. By noon some two thousand students had assembled at one end of the campus Commons; on the opposite end, National Guard troops gathered in formation.

Ordering the protesters to disperse, the National Guardsmen advanced and fired tear gas canisters in an effort to break up the crowd. The students countered by throwing rocks at the guardsmen. Suddenly, one guardsman opened fire on the students. Several others began shooting, and in the space of thirteen seconds, sixty-seven shots were fired. When the smoke cleared, four students were dead, and nine others lay wounded.

The Kent State shootings prompted protests at colleges throughout the United States, forcing many campuses to close. An official investigation of the incident concluded that the guardsmen were not justified in firing on the students. A campus memorial now commemorates the tragic events of May 4, 1970.

Journalists covering the Tet Offensive began to see differences between the official combat reports and what was actually occurring on the battlefield. Television coverage of the war soon became less optimistic and more skeptical of the information that was coming from the generals in the field. Throughout his tour as commander in Vietnam, Westmoreland had made positive statements such as, "I am optimistic and we are making good progress," and, "At the present time I believe the whole operation is moving in our favor."[30] After Tet, even Westmoreland, who insisted that he had anticipated the invasion, grudgingly admitted, "The offensive revealed an unexpected determination by North Vietnam to pursue the war regardless of price."[31]

Film footage from Vietnam after Tet began to include more scenes that depicted the brutality of the war. To emphasize the human side of the war, television journalists began to balance the cold casualty statistics with more stories of the men involved in the fighting. Footage of the fight for the American embassy in Saigon showed the bodies of the Vietcong insurgents killed by US soldiers. Editorial pieces, which before Tet had been mostly positive about America's role in the war, began to present a more pessimistic view of US involvement and the now uncertain possibility of victory in Vietnam. For the first time, television viewers were seeing the violence of the war as it actually was.

> "The [Tet] offensive revealed an unexpected determination by North Vietnam to pursue the war regardless of price."[31]
>
> —General William Westmoreland

Cronkite at War

In the 1960s most Americans got their news from what were, at the time, the only major television networks: ABC, CBS, and NBC. Of all the network news anchors, Walter Cronkite of CBS was the most respected by American audiences. Often referred to as "the most trusted man in America," Cronkite's sincerity on the air, as well as his war reporting skills honed in World War II, lent authority to his nightly reports on Vietnam that other news anchors could not equal. In February 1968 while the Tet Offensive was still going on, Cronkite flew to Vietnam with a camera crew to view the progress of the war firsthand. He traveled through most of South Vietnam, observing marines fighting in the streets of Hue and watched as US bombs and rockets pounded suspected enemy positions outside of Saigon. He talked with both grunts (ordinary foot soldiers) and generals commanding the American combat operations. Cronkite soon began to realize that the reports coming from military leaders indicating that the war would soon be over were at best exaggerations, and at worst outright lies.

Upon his return to the United States, Cronkite produced a prime-time special entitled *Report from Vietnam*, which aired on February 27, 1968. To an audience of millions, he described the progress of the war, using film clips of combat operations. At the end of the program, Cronkite changed from objective reporter to editorial commentator. As he looked intently into the camera, and into America's homes, his final words had a profound effect on the attitudes of ordinary citizens toward the war:

> Who won and who lost in the great Tet Offensive against the cities? I'm not sure. The Vietcong did not win by a knockout, but neither did we. . . . We have been too often disappointed by the optimism of the American leaders, both in Vietnam and in Washington, to have faith any longer in the silver linings they find in the darkest clouds. . . . For it seems now more certain than ever that the bloody experience of Vietnam is to end in a stalemate.[32]

CBS broadcast journalist Walter Cronkite (center) conducts an interview in Hue during the Tet Offensive. His reporting enabled Americans at home to witness the violence and brutality of the war.

The impact of Cronkite's televised statements were far reaching. According to journalist David Halberstam, "It was the first time in American history a war had been declared over by an anchorman."[33]

A legend has grown up around Johnson's reaction to the broadcast. After hearing Cronkite's closing remarks, Johnson reportedly lamented, "If I've lost Cronkite, I've lost middle America."[34] Other television journalists began questioning the progress of the war in the wake of Tet. Frank McGee of NBC told his audience, "The grand objective—the building of a free nation—is not nearer but further from realization. In short, the war, as the Administration has defined it, is being lost."[35] Public opinion was especially harsh when it came to Johnson's handling of the war. At the end of 1967, his overall approval rating had been 49 percent; by March 1968 it had dropped to 36 percent. As Johnson feared, he had indeed lost middle America.

> "For it seems now more certain than ever that the bloody experience of Vietnam is to end in a stalemate."[32]
>
> —CBS journalist Walter Cronkite

The Importance of Tet

Ten years after the Vietnam War ended, Cronkite stood before a large map of Southeast Asia in a CBS TV studio, recalling the turning point of the war. "If you had to choose the most important event of the Vietnam War, it certainly would be the Tet Offensive. It changed how people looked at the war, and in doing so changed the war itself."[36] With those words, Cronkite summed up the importance of Tet. Throughout the war, American military leaders had been encouraging the idea that Communist defeats were a sign that the war would soon be over. Just a month before the Tet Offensive, Walt Rostow, Johnson's national security advisor, proclaimed that NVA and Vietcong "casualties are going up at a rate they cannot sustain. I see light at the end of the tunnel."[37] The aftermath of Tet, however, proved just the opposite: that despite horrendous losses, the Communist forces were able to bounce back and continue their fight for liberation.

After Tet the military's optimistic reports about the progress of the war were revealed by the media to be merely attempts to put a positive spin on a losing cause. These revelations further eroded public opinion. By the time US involvement in the war ended in 1973, 60 percent of Americans thought sending US troops to Vietnam had been a mistake. The term *credibility gap* was first used in 1965 to explain the rift between the American people and their leaders concerning the Vietnam War. Historian James H. Willbanks notes that "the political ramifications of [the Tet Offensive] widened the credibility gap and further shook the confidence of the American people in their president and his war effort."[38]

After Tet, 1968 would go on to become the bloodiest year of the war, with US forces suffering more than 16,500 killed. But there were other casualties as well. Johnson, battered by a losing war and plummeting public opinion, declined to run for a second term. For his handling of Tet, Westmoreland was removed as commander of US forces in Vietnam. The loss of US and South Vietnamese troops, along with thousands of civilian deaths, can never be reversed. But perhaps the greatest losses to America were the shattering of national unity and the damage inflicted on the public's trust in its military and government leaders.

CHAPTER FOUR

How Did Richard Nixon's Policies Influence the War's Outcome?

Focus Questions

1. What was the rationale behind Nixon's strategy of Vietnamization, and how well did it work? What other options did he have for ending the war?
2. Is government secrecy in matters of war ever justified? Describe the circumstances under which secrecy might and might not be justified.
3. What does the statement "peace with honor" mean, and why did Nixon make this his stated goal?

On August 5, 1968, the Republican Party opened its national convention at the Miami Beach Convention Center in Florida. Richard Nixon, who had been vice president under Dwight D. Eisenhower, was the leading contender for the nomination. On the campaign trail, Nixon had promised that, if elected president, he would restore law and order in America, strengthen the economy, and bring an end to the Vietnam War. Before throngs of delegates cheering and holding Nixon for President signs, Nixon received his party's nomination. In his acceptance speech, he declared, "I pledge to you tonight that the first priority foreign policy objective of our next Administration will be to bring an honorable end to the war in Vietnam."[39]

Two months later Nixon was elected president, defeating Democrat Hubert Humphrey. The news of Nixon's election hit the newspapers the next morning with bold headlines and hopeful editorials about what the new president might accomplish in the Oval Office.

Pushed off the front page was less-encouraging news from halfway around the world: On election day, twenty-seven more Americans had died in Vietnam.

Vietnamization

On numerous occasions during his presidential campaign, Nixon vowed that he would bring an honorable end to the war in Vietnam, but he provided no specifics as to how the United States would ac-

complish this. After taking the oath of office on January 20, 1969, Nixon had to transform his words into a plan of action. At the beginning of 1969, there were approximately 542,000 American troops in Vietnam. Nixon's job was to bring the troops home quickly enough to satisfy an American public that was growing more disillusioned with each new casualty report. At the same time, he knew that withdrawing all the troops immediately would mean abandoning America's pledge to aid South Vietnam, leaving it vulnerable to a Communist takeover. He feared it would also destroy US credibility with its numerous allies around the world.

Nixon's plan, which actually originated with his secretary of defense, Melvin Laird, was called Vietnamization. It called for gradually bringing US troops home, while providing more modern weapons and air support to allow the ARVN to assume the burden of conducting the war. As Nixon later explained in his book *No More Vietnams*:

The key new element in our strategy was a plan for the complete withdrawal of all American combat troops from Vietnam. Americans needed tangible evidence that we were winding down the war, and the South Vietnamese needed to be given more responsibility for their defense. We were not pulling out according to a fixed schedule. . . . As South Vietnamese forces became stronger, the rate of American withdrawal could become greater. The announcement of the withdrawal program made another subtle but profoundly important point: While the French had fought to stay in Vietnam, the United States was fighting to get out.[40]

On June 8, 1969, Nixon introduced Vietnamization by declaring that 25,000 US troops would be withdrawn from Vietnam by the end of August. It was the first of several troop withdrawals over the next year and a half; 35,000 more would come home by December 15, another 50,000 by April 1970, and 150,000 additional troops would be withdrawn by the end of 1970. Vietnamization would be complete when all US troops had left the war-torn country. "The time has come,"

A Communist sympathizer travels along the Ho Chi Minh Trail in the early 1970s. This route, a network of trails camouflaged by thick jungle cover, made possible the delivery of weapons and supplies to Vietcong fighting in the South.

Nixon said, "to end this war. Let history record at this critical moment, both sides turned their faces toward peace rather than toward conflict and war."[41] But while Nixon was disengaging US soldiers from Vietnam, he was secretly expanding the war past Vietnam's western border.

Bombing Cambodia

Vietnam's immediate neighbors, Cambodia and Laos, had declared themselves neutral parties in the war between the North and South. This meant that ground troops for either side were forbidden from operating in those countries. Both, however, allowed North Vietnam to create a supply route that ran along their eastern borders with North and South Vietnam. The route, called the Ho Chi Minh Trail, consisted of a network of footpaths, bicycle trails, and dirt roads all camouflaged by thick jungle cover. The route expedited the delivery of weapons and supplies to Vietcong fighting in the South; by 1965 hundreds of tons of supplies were being transported south over the Ho Chi Minh Trail every day.

Although professing to be neutral, Cambodia's head of state, Prince Norodom Sihanouk, was actually sympathetic to the North's cause. He believed the Communists would eventually win the war. Along with allowing the Ho Chi Minh Trail to run through his country, Sihanouk permitted North Vietnam to build supply depots, training camps, and troop sanctuaries on Cambodian soil. Using these bases, Vietcong soldiers could cross the border into South Vietnam, strike at their targets, and scramble back to safety in Cambodia. It was from these sanctuaries that Communist troops crossed the border in February 1969 to begin a new ground assault that lasted for more than three months. Nixon took this new offensive as a personal affront, a test of his strength as the new president. "We cannot tolerate one more of these [assaults in South Vietnam] without hitting back,"[42] Nixon declared.

Nixon's decision to hit back came in the form of an intense bombing campaign. Called Operation Menu, the campaign's mission was to target Communist sanctuaries in Cambodia, including a Communist headquarters that was believed to be hidden there. But retaliation presented a problem for the president: Escalating the conflict into another country while at the same time advocating a peaceful end to

The Nixon Doctrine

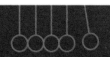

With the Vietnam War placing an increasing burden on America's military and financial resources, Richard Nixon sought a better way to continue to honor America's commitments to its allies. The result was a new direction in US foreign policy, which would become known as the Nixon Doctrine. In a televised address on November 3, 1969, Nixon explained the basic tenets of this doctrine to the American people:

> First, the United States will keep all of its treaty commitments.

> Second, we shall provide a shield if a nuclear power threatens the freedom of a nation allied with us or of a nation whose survival we consider vital to our security.

> Third, in cases involving other types of aggression, we shall furnish military and economic assistance when requested in accordance with our treaty commitments. But we shall look to the nation directly threatened to assume the primary responsibility of providing the manpower for its defense.

With the mounting US casualties of the Vietnam War in mind, Nixon was pledging that the United States would continue to support its allies, especially in Asia, with economic aid and military equipment but without sending in ground combat troops. The Nixon Doctrine heralded a shift in US foreign policy, attempting to end the bilateral superpower conflict between the United States and the Soviet Union and move toward sharing the responsibility for world peace among all major nations.

Richard Nixon, "Address to the Nation on the War in Vietnam," American Presidency Project, November 3, 1969. www.presidency.ucsb.edu.

the war would surely spark new antiwar demonstrations at home. So Nixon ordered the bombing to be carried out in strictest secrecy. "No comment, no warnings, no complaints, no protests," he cautioned National Security Advisor Henry Kissinger in a telephone conversation on March 15, 1969, just days before the bombers were scheduled to begin their strikes. "I mean it, not one thing to be said to anyone publicly or privately without my prior approval."[43]

Over its fourteen-month duration, Operation Menu bombers dropped more than 100 tons (91 metric tons) of bombs on suspected Communist targets in Cambodia. But it did little to curtail the flow of Communist troops from Cambodia into South Vietnam. Nixon, however, had another objective for the bombing operation. By showing US willingness to use its military might, he hoped to convince North Vietnam to return to the bargaining table at the Paris peace talks, which had collapsed into a frustrating stalemate.

Troubled Talks in Paris

Peace negotiations had begun in 1968 during the Johnson administration. On May 10 delegations representing the opposing nations sat down at a large table to try to bring an end to the war. From the beginning, the negotiations stalled over seemingly insurmountable differences. The United States demanded that all North Vietnamese troops withdraw from South Vietnam, which the North would not agree to. The North would not negotiate unless the Vietcong were included in the talks, a condition that the US resisted. Neither side wavered from its demands, and the North Vietnamese vowed to stay at the negotiating table "until the chairs rot."[44]

After taking office, Nixon became frustrated by the lack of progress in Paris. On July 15, 1969, he sent a letter to Ho Chi Minh in which he stated, "I deeply believe that the war in Vietnam has gone on too long and delay in bringing it to an end can benefit no one—least of all the people of Vietnam. . . . The time has come to move forward at the conference table toward an early resolution of this tragic war."[45] Ho's reply accused the United States of waging a war of aggression against the Vietnamese people and restated the North's position that only total US withdrawal from Vietnam would end the war.

While the talks stalled in Paris, in the US antiwar protests continued. October 15, 1969, was declared National Moratorium Day, and millions of people all across the country participated in nonviolent protest activities. Despite the growing number of demonstrations against the war, Nixon was convinced that most Americans supported his plan for ending the war. In a nationally televised speech on November 3,

Nixon used a term that would come to describe the ordinary citizen. "I know it may not be fashionable to speak of patriotism or national destiny these days," Nixon said. "But I feel it is appropriate to do so on this occasion.... And so tonight—to you, the great silent majority of my fellow Americans—I ask for your support."[46] Nixon's "silent majority" did not attend demonstrations or join the radical counterculture, but its opinions were no less important than those of the protesters who had captured the media spotlight. After the speech, Nixon's approval ratings skyrocketed, proof that the silent majority had indeed been listening.

Operation Duck Hook

President Nixon was bluffing with his so-called madman scheme when he sent bombers loaded with nuclear weapons flying just outside the Soviet border. It was a dangerous ruse, but it raises a chilling question: Did Nixon ever seriously consider using nuclear weapons to end the Vietnam War? According to classified documents released in 2005, the answer is yes, he did.

The three presidents before Nixon—Eisenhower, Kennedy, and Johnson—had all considered the use of nuclear weapons but rejected the idea for reasons ranging from moral grounds to the possibility of starting a nuclear war with the Soviet Union. Upon taking office, Nixon wanted to keep his campaign promise of ending the war, and he issued threats of increased military action to persuade North Vietnam to end its stalling at the Paris peace talks. But mere threats were having little success, so in July 1969 Nixon and his national security advisor, Henry Kissinger, came up with an alternative: Operation Duck Hook.

The plan called for a massive assault on North Vietnam, including air strikes on several important military and industrial targets near Hanoi, using nuclear weapons. Operation Duck Hook was abandoned before it could be implemented, due to concerns from some of Nixon's top advisors and the possible public relations nightmare from such a bold escalation of the war.

Could Vietnam have escalated to an all-out nuclear war between the world's superpowers? Fortunately, the answer remains forever in the realm of speculation.

Madman Nixon

Nixon had promised an end to the war, but with peace talks at a stand-still, he decided to try a different tactic. He decided to publicly portray himself as a madman who would pursue any and all avenues—including the use of nuclear weapons—to halt the war. Nixon had come up with the madman ploy during his presidential campaign. As he explained in 1968 to his chief of staff H.R. "Bob" Haldeman, the idea was to get Ho to take the need for negotiation seriously enough to agree to a diplomatic solution to the war:

> I call it the madman theory, Bob. I want the North Vietnamese to believe I've reached the point where I might do *anything* to stop the war. We'll just slip the word to them that, "for God's sake, you know Nixon is obsessed about Communism. We can't restrain him when he's angry—and he has his hand on the nuclear button"—and Ho Chi Minh will be in Paris in two days begging for peace.[47]

To reinforce his point, Nixon ordered eighteen B-52 bombers armed with nuclear weapons to fly across the Pacific toward North Vietnam's top benefactor, the Soviet Union. For three days, under Operation Giant Lance, the bombers flew just outside Soviet airspace, taunting the Soviets in a dangerous game of cat and mouse. Anatoly Dobrynin, the Soviet ambassador to the United States, immediately contacted Nixon to demand an end to these provocative actions. Nixon responded with a threat: "The United States reserves the right to go its own way and to use its own methods to end the war." The methods he was referring to clearly included nuclear attack on the Soviet Union. Dobrynin reported to his superiors, "Nixon is unable to control himself even in a conversation with a foreign ambassador."[48] Nixon's portrayal as a madman seemed to be working.

After three days Operation Giant Lance ended as abruptly as it began, and the B-52s returned home. This quick withdrawal reinforced the notion that Nixon was unstable, seeming to risk starting a nuclear war on a whim and then impulsively pulling back his threat. But the campaign neither persuaded North Vietnam to negotiate nor convinced the Soviet Union to end its support of the Communists in the war. Although

Giant Lance failed, Nixon had another secret weapon he planned to unleash on Vietnam: his national security advisor, Henry Kissinger.

Back-Channel Negotiations

With official diplomatic talks at a stalemate, Nixon and Kissinger knew they would have to find another way to negotiate. The president charged Kissinger with arranging and conducting secret, or back-channel, negotiations. On August 4, 1969, Kissinger had his first meeting outside Paris with Le Duc Tho, who was acting as special counselor to North Vietnam's official delegation. Over the next several years, talks between Kissinger and Tho resulted in no more success than did the official talks in Paris.

While the secret negotiations were going on, Nixon planned his own dramatic mission to help bring peace to Vietnam. Since the Communist takeover in 1949, relations between the United States and China had become chilly. Nixon believed he could thaw those relations with a personal visit to China. By meeting with Chinese premier Zhou Enlai, the president hoped to weaken the Communist nation's support

US president Richard Nixon (left) dines with Chinese premier Zhou Enlai in 1972. Nixon's visit was an attempt to improve relations between the United States and China and persuade its leaders to weaken their support of North Vietnam.

for North Vietnam. At the same time, relations between China and the Soviet Union were also strained. If Nixon could bring the United States and China closer together, the Soviet Union might be more inclined to influence the peace negotiations in Paris. "Instead of using Vietnam to contain China," commented historian Walter LaFeber, "Nixon concluded that he had better use China to contain Vietnam."[49]

Nixon arrived in Beijing on February 21, 1972, the first US president to visit the Communist country. During the seven-day trip, he discussed a number of topics with Zhou and Mao, visited the Great Wall of China, and attended banquets that were televised in the United States. Photographs of the leaders of the two great nations, smiling and engaging in conversation, flashed around the world. By the time Nixon returned home, relations between China and the United States had improved, and Nixon's legacy as a statesman was assured. But there was no change in China's attitude toward the Vietnam War. Zhou told Nixon, "So long as you continue your practice of Vietnamization . . . and so long as the Vietnamese, the [Laotians], and the Cambodians continue to fight, we will not stop supporting them for a single day."[50]

> "Instead of using Vietnam to contain China, Nixon concluded that he had better use China to contain Vietnam."[49]
>
> —Historian Walter LaFeber

Breakthrough

While Vietnamization continued, so did the fighting. On March 30, 1972, the NVA launched an operation called the Easter Offensive. Some two hundred thousand NVA troops invaded South Vietnam in a last-ditch effort to win an all-out victory. In response, Nixon ordered a massive bombing raid against North Vietnam and the mining of its harbors to prevent arms shipments from reaching the North. The Easter Offensive lasted until October, when both sides, exhausted from the bitter fighting, halted their combat efforts. But by then, the peace talks in Paris were finally making some progress.

During the secret negotiations in early October, Kissinger and Tho completed a draft of an agreement that would end the war. On October 26, 1972, Kissinger announced the breakthrough, saying, "We

During the Easter Offensive, President Nixon ordered a massive bombing raid (pictured is an aerial view of US Air Force and Navy planes dropping bombs) against North Vietnam.

believe that peace is at hand."[51] This came at an opportune moment for Nixon, who was campaigning for a second term in the November elections, just a week away. But it was also premature: Nguyen Van Thieu, South Vietnam's president, was angered that the agreement allowed NVA soldiers to remain in South Vietnam. Thieu proposed sixty-nine changes to the agreement, which North Vietnamese negotiators rejected.

Nixon reassured Thieu that the United States would continue to support South Vietnam. To confirm that support—and to send a message to North Vietnam that the United States was serious about it—he ordered increased bombing of the North. Formal negotiations eventually resumed, and on January 23, 1973, Nixon announced that "we today have concluded an agreement to end the war and bring peace with honor."[52] Four days later, representatives from North and South Vietnam, the Vietcong, and the United States signed the peace treaty, ending the Vietnam War.

> "We today have concluded an agreement to end the war and bring peace with honor."[52]
>
> —US president Richard Nixon

For Nixon, ending the war became a part of his presidential legacy. With US troops gone from Vietnam, however, the North began preparations to finally unite North and South under communism. Nixon had given his word to Thieu that the United States would help South Vietnam against any further aggression from the North. But by the time NVA tanks rolled through the streets of Saigon in April 1975, US support had not materialized, and Thieu surrendered his nation to communism. Nixon may have ended the war, but his peace with honor was too fragile to survive.

CHAPTER FIVE

What Lasting Impact Did the Vietnam War Have on the United States and Vietnam?

Focus Questions

1. Do you believe the United States had—or still has—a responsibility to help rebuild Vietnam? Why or why not?
2. How did the Vietnam War affect public attitudes toward the US military and political leaders, and do these attitudes persist? Explain your answer.
3. What effect did the Vietnam War have on US policies regarding involvement in other wars, and are these policies a benefit or a detriment to the United States?

The image is at once dramatic and heartbreaking. A US helicopter sits precariously on the rooftop elevator shaft of an apartment building in Saigon, a gathering point for South Vietnamese fleeing the approach of Communist troops on April 29, 1975. In the photograph a long line of evacuees snakes up a ladder to the roof, each person desperately hoping to get on the aircraft before it takes off.

Fifteen people managed to board the helicopter, which was designed to carry only eight passengers. Then, its rotors beating the air, it lifted skyward to fly its human cargo to the safety of a waiting US aircraft carrier. More rescue flights from other gathering points took place over the next eight hours. After delivering their passengers, many of the choppers were pushed overboard to make room for more incoming aircraft. The next day, April 30, North Vietnamese tanks rolled into Saigon, ending the Vietnam War and uniting the nation under communism. In his book *In Retrospect*, Robert

McNamara, secretary of defense during most of the Johnson administration, writes, "Results are what we expect, consequences are what we get."[53] With the fall of Saigon, the results hoped for at the beginning of the war turned into unexpected consequences that had a profound effect on both the United States and Vietnam.

The Human Cost of War

The cost in lives of the Vietnam War can be calculated with cold precision; 58,220 Americans died in the jungles of Vietnam, more than were killed in World War I or the Korean War. But statistics cannot portray the pain of losing a husband, brother, or father in a war that most Americans felt was unjust and incompetently conducted by the government. "I was angry at the government for many years," relates Barbara Sonneborn, whose husband, Jeff, died in Vietnam. "When Jeff was killed, I never blamed the Vietnamese people. I blamed the government for their folly, for their mistakes, for their misuse of a generation of young men. I felt outside our culture."[54]

"When Jeff was killed, I never blamed the Vietnamese people. I blamed the government for their folly, for their mistakes, for their misuse of a generation of young men."[54]

—Barbara Sonneborn, widow of a soldier killed in Vietnam

The pain of loss is not restricted to Americans. North Vietnamese mother Pham an Dau lost four of her five sons in the war. "I didn't know how they had died," she said in a 2015 interview with a BBC journalist. "I didn't know what they were doing when they died. I just knew that they were gone. Losing a child is the greatest sadness."[55] The death toll of Vietnamese is staggering. Although exact statistics are difficult to obtain, according to numerous sources including the Vietnamese government, as many as 3.8 million Vietnamese lost their lives during the conflict—including some 2 million civilians. Many thousands more died in neighboring Cambodia and Laos.

Some of these deaths were the result of atrocities. Targeted assassinations of people thought to be aiding the enemy effort were committed by both the United States and the North Vietnamese. Often due to faulty intelligence, many innocent people were murdered

Vietnamese refugees fleeing Communist troops board a US aircraft carrier during the evacuation of Saigon in April 1975. Shortly afterward the capital fell to North Vietnamese forces.

under these programs. The village of Dak Son was destroyed by the Vietcong in December 1967 and the entire population killed or abducted. In the occupied city of Hue during the Tet Offensive in 1968, NVA troops massacred as many as six thousand South Vietnamese military officials, civil servants, and ordinary citizens. Their bodies were later discovered in mass graves. In March 1968 American troops under the orders of Lieutenant William Calley killed between three hundred and five hundred civilians—men, women, and children—in the village of My Lai.

The deaths of innocent people did not stop with the end of the war. In May 2016 the *New Yorker* magazine published an article with

The suffering of the Vietnamese people, especially in the South, did not stop when the war ended in 1975. After the Communists had united the two Vietnams, economic hardships and the possibility of suffering the same prejudice and oppression that had occurred in other Communist-subjugated nations created a rising fear among the South Vietnamese. In 1978 a wave of Vietnamese sought to escape. They boarded small boats in hopes of finding refuge in other countries of Southeast Asia. These refugees were called "boat people," and their journeys to freedom were fraught with hardships.

Many people sold all of their possessions to pay the bribes necessary to gain approval from local authorities to leave Vietnam. Once at sea, other perils threatened their journey. The boats were overcrowded, and there was little or no food or water for the passengers. Pirates brutally attacked the refugees, and rough seas and sudden storms threatened to capsize the rickety vessels. Once the boat people landed, usually in Malaysia, Singapore, or Thailand, they faced hostility from the local population, who resented the influx of so many foreigners. The receiving nations ultimately reached an agreement with the UN that if they allowed the boat people to land, the UN would settle the refugees in other nations such as the United States and Canada.

According to UN estimates, some 800,000 boat people escaped Vietnam's Communist regime and resettled in other nations. An estimated 200,000 to 250,000 perished on the journey.

a provocative title: "The Vietnam War Is Still Killing People." According to the author, George Black, more than forty years after the war ended, unexploded bombs, artillery shells, and other live munitions buried across the nation continue to present a danger to the Vietnamese people. Black describes the problem:

> Since the end of the war, in 1975, more than forty thousand Vietnamese have been killed by [unexploded ordnance]. . . . A naval shell turns up in an irrigation ditch, or a couple of hand grenades are found at the edge of a rice paddy. Perhaps an artil-

lery round gets unearthed by a construction crew digging the foundations for a new house. Just this past week, a gigantic thousand-pound bomb, almost seven feet long, was discovered by workers digging a drainage tunnel in Quang Tri township.[56]

More than three-quarters of the Vietnamese population live in rural areas, where farming is the lifeblood of the people. After the war many Vietnamese farmers tried to resume their livelihood, only to discover that their rice paddies could no longer be planted due to the danger of munitions that could be detonated with the step of an ox or the blade of a plow. Other farmland was rendered unsuitable for cultivation due to destructive US bombing raids carried out throughout the war. Although the Paris Peace Accords officially ended hostilities, the Vietnam War held more anguish for both the Vietnamese and the Americans who had fought in their land.

Chemical Legacy

One of the most destructive legacies of the Vietnam War was the US operation to destroy jungle vegetation by the use of chemicals called defoliants. Throughout the war North Vietnamese forces used the lush jungles of Vietnam to their advantage: The all-encompassing foliage obscured troop movements and provided cover from which the NVA and Vietcong could ambush US and ARVN soldiers. In 1962 the United States initiated Operation Ranch Hand, a systematic program of spreading defoliants across the Vietnamese countryside by spraying them from low-flying aircraft. The purpose of the operation was twofold: to deny the enemy its means of hiding and to destroy its crops.

Several types of defoliants were used in Operation Ranch Hand, each identified by a colored stripe on its 55-gallon (208-L) drum container. The most widely used defoliant employed during the operation was called Agent Orange, a mixture of two chemical defoliants. Beginning in 1962, US cargo aircraft and helicopters flying just above tree level sprayed Agent Orange over wide swaths of South Vietnam, often coming close to US camps. Most US troops did not know the purpose of the operation. As former army medic John Green recalls, "I really didn't know what they were spraying. Some people thought it was for mosquitoes, but I never really gave it much thought. . . . I do remember walking through the defoliated zones. Everything was dead. . . . Some of our food was undoubtedly sprayed with Agent Orange. But how were we to know? The army told us the stuff was harmless."[57]

Agent Orange was anything but harmless. One of its component chemicals contained dioxin, a highly toxic, cancer-causing substance. The deadly effects of dioxin spared neither Americans nor Vietnamese. From 1962 to 1971 Operation Ranch Hand aircraft dispersed some 19 million gallons (72 million L) of defoliant, of which about 12 million gallons (45.4 million L) were Agent Orange. More than 5 million acres (2.02 ha) of forests were affected by the operation. "The loss of a significant proportion of southern Vietnam's forest cover triggered a number of related effects," says Dr. Wayne Dwernychuk, an expert on Agent Orange. "Loss of timber led to reduced sustainability of ecosystems, decreases in the biodiversity of plants and animals, poorer soil quality, [and] increased water contamination."[58] It has been estimated that it would likely take up to one hundred years for the forests to grow back to their prewar condition. Defoliation also destroyed the habitats of numerous animal species, including tigers, elephants, and water buffalo. But the chemical devastation was not limited to the land alone.

> "Some of our food was undoubtedly sprayed with Agent Orange. But how were we to know? The army told us the stuff was harmless."[57]
>
> —John Green, US Army medic in Vietnam

An estimated 4.8 million South Vietnamese villagers and 1 million North and South Vietnam soldiers were affected by Agent Orange, suffering from disorders that ranged from lung diseases, infertility, and birth defects to skin rashes and cancer. Effects of the defoliant lingered long after the fighting ended, with children often becoming innocent victims. Do Duc Diu, a North Vietnam soldier, was stationed in an area that was sprayed with Agent Orange. After the war, Diu and his wife had fifteen children, twelve of whom died before age three from diseases likely related to Agent Orange exposure. Diu visits their graves nearly every day. "I can say that I have no future, no happiness,"[59] he laments.

Thousands of US troops who fought in Vietnam were also victims of Operation Ranch Hand, and the effects of Agent Orange continue

A US military helicopter sprays a defoliant on a dense jungle area during Operation Ranch Hand. US troops and Vietnamese soldiers and civilians who were exposed to Agent Orange, the most widely used defoliant, continue to suffer its deadly effects decades later.

to cause suffering decades after the veterans' service ended. Terry Stinson, an air force mechanic in Vietnam from 1970 to 1971, contracted diabetes due to Agent Orange exposure. "I started showing signs when I was 26 years old," Stinson recalls. "Now, here I am 64 years old and I'm taking seven insulin shots a day. . . . I can't feel my feet anymore."[60] Stinson is only one of some 2.8 million US soldiers, sailors, and air personnel exposed to Agent Orange.

For years the Veterans Administration (now the US Department of Veterans Affairs) denied compensation to Vietnam veterans who reported being affected by Agent Orange, due to the difficulty of connecting their diseases to the defoliant. In 1991 the Agent Orange Act confirmed that certain diseases were related to dioxin exposure, paving the way for thousands of Vietnam veterans to receive disability payments. These veterans are now compensated for cancers, diabetes, and heart problems due to Agent Orange exposure. But many Vietnam veterans suffer from another disorder that is harder to diagnose but is just as deadly.

A Lasting Trauma

It has been called by many names in many wars: soldier's heart in the Civil War, shell shock in World War I, combat fatigue in World War II. Today it is known as post-traumatic stress disorder (PTSD), and some 11 percent of Vietnam veterans—more than 270,000 men and women—suffer from its effects. PTSD is a psychological disorder that results from experiencing an extremely stressful situation, often life threatening in nature. A person with PTSD may experience anxiety, nightmares, jumpiness, alienation from friends or loved ones, and flashbacks (reliving traumatic events). Leading a normal life is nearly impossible when PTSD symptoms may appear at any time. PTSD victims may find it difficult to hold down a job, can be withdrawn in social situations, and may have difficulty maintaining healthy family relationships. Veteran Dan Rihn describes his own struggle with PTSD:

> "Vietnam left me with a constant inner agitation I can't fully understand. . . . I lash out at people. I lose my temper quickly. Little things upset me—things most people wouldn't think twice about."[61]
>
> —Vietnam veteran Dan Rihn, who struggles with PTSD

Vietnam left me with a constant inner agitation I can't fully understand, let alone describe with clarity. I lash out at people. I lose my temper quickly. Little things upset me—things most people wouldn't think twice about. There are times when I want to hurt someone even though that someone doesn't have either a name or a face—it doesn't matter, just as long as I can think about hurting someone seems to provide some level of comfort or satisfaction. I believe this inner irritation or agitation is the direct result of my time in Nam.[61]

Treatment for PTSD includes various types of counseling and therapy, as well as medications that can relieve the depression and anxiety associated with the disorder. Although no statistics are available, it is fairly likely that numerous Vietnamese soldiers and citizens

Vietnam's New Economy

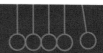

More than forty years after Ho Chi Minh's vision of a united Vietnam was realized, the Communists still hold virtually unchallenged political power. Radio and television are regulated by the government, and Internet sites that oppose the regime are blocked. But when it comes to business, Vietnam is quickly becoming a major player in the twenty-first-century global economy. According to the BBC, Vietnam's economy got off to a slow start.

> Vietnam struggled to find its feet after unification and tried at first to organise the agricultural economy along strict state-run lines. But elements of market forces and private enterprise were introduced from the late 1980s and a stock exchange opened in 2000. Foreign investment has grown and the US is Vietnam's main trading partner. In the cities, the consumer market is fueled by the appetite of a young, middle class for electronic and luxury goods.

> Vietnam's economy is gaining strength. It is now the second-largest supplier of shoes worldwide, exporting more than 1 billion footwear products per year. Vietnam exported more than $35 billion worth of goods to the United States in 2016, including apparel, shoes, electronic products, seafood, and machinery. Global investment firm Goldman Sachs predicts that Vietnam's economy, which ranked fifty-fifth in 2015, will become the seventeenth largest in the world by 2025.

"Vietnam Profile—Overview," BBC News, January 27, 2016. www.bbc.com.

also suffer from PTSD. In Orange County, California, where many Vietnamese refugees relocated after the war, clinics treat symptoms of PTSD in older Vietnamese refugees. "Post traumatic stress is very prevalent in the community," says Paul Hoang, an Orange County social worker. "My dad has it, I had it, I was a refugee."[62]

A Different America

PTSD has had a profound effect on the personal lives of those who have it. The Vietnam War also had a profound effect on the American public. Americans suffered a crisis of confidence in their government as a result of this war, which is forever linked to official falsehoods and half-truths. Numerous optimistic statements from military leaders that the US was nearing victory were countered by scenes of fierce combat that appeared nightly on television. By the end of the war, and in the years that followed, Americans began questioning whether they could actually trust their government.

Although the war was drawing to a close in the 1970s, that decade marked a challenging period in US history. Inflation, soaring gas prices, and the need for two-paycheck households to make ends meet placed a burden, both financially and psychologically, on American families. Disillusioned by the government's handling of the war, Americans had little faith that their leaders could fix these problems. In 1976 presidential candidate Jimmy Carter told the American people, "In recent years, our nation has seen a failure of leadership. We've been hurt and we're disillusioned. We've seen a wall go up that separates us from our government. . . . It's now a time for healing. . . . It's time for the people to run the government, and not the other way around."[63] Carter was elected in no small part because voters perceived him as being an outsider to the Washington establishment and hoped he would bring accountability to American politics.

Waging War and the Vietnam Syndrome

Not only politics, but diplomatic and military policies were altered by the war. After Vietnam, America changed the way it interacted with other nations, especially militarily. In 1973 Congress enacted the War Powers Resolution requiring a president to notify Congress within forty-eight hours of committing armed forces to a military conflict.

Exhausted US Marines wait for their helicopter airlift by the DMZ in 1968. In addition to the thousands killed in the Vietnam War, more than 270,000 veterans have suffered the effects of PTSD.

The War Powers Resolution has influenced the way troops have been deployed since Vietnam. In 1983 President Ronald Reagan sought congressional approval to send US Marines to Lebanon. President George H.W. Bush asked Congress in 1991 for permission to begin Operation Desert Storm in response to Iraq's invasion of Kuwait. Although it has been debated and criticized since its inception, the intent of the War Powers Resolution has always been to keep the United States out of another Vietnam.

By 1980 America was trying its best to put Vietnam behind it, but it was not easy to forget a decade of bloodshed and suffering. Historian Alexander Bloom describes a new attitude that had taken over the American psyche:

Over the last quarter of the twentieth century and the first decade of the twenty-first century, the shadow of Vietnam continued to hang over American life, from U.S. foreign policy and domestic politics to the personal attitudes of individual American citizens. This haunting aura of the war in Indochina took on a name of its own—the "Vietnam Syndrome"—describing the cynical, frustrated, and pessimistic sense with which America approached the world.[64]

The Vietnam Syndrome had a particular effect on the way the military establishment viewed its role in international conflicts. The fact that America had suffered a humiliating loss at the hands of a third-world nation shook the confidence of the military leaders and political policymakers whose job it was to decide what wars the nation was obligated to fight. Journalist and television news analyst Marvin Kalb describes the Vietnam Syndrome as "a fundamental reluctance to commit American military power anywhere in the world, unless it is absolutely necessary to protect the national interests of this country."[65]

Even decades after its end, the two nations most affected by the war, the United States and Vietnam, still suffer from its effects. The memory of the war is reflected today in the black granite walls of the Vietnam Veterans Memorial in Washington, DC; in the scarred landscape of Vietnam; and in the hearts and minds of the people of two nations forever changed by war.

> "This haunting aura of the war in Indochina took on a name of its own—the 'Vietnam Syndrome'—describing the cynical, frustrated, and pessimistic sense with which America approached the world."[64]
>
> —Historian Alexander Bloom

Introduction: Fighting for Independence

1. Declaration of Independence, National Archives. www.archives .gov.
2. Ho Chi Minh, "Declaration of Independence of the Democratic Republic of Viet-Nam, September 2, 1945," Mt Holyoke College. www.mtholyoke.edu.

Chapter One: A Brief History of the Vietnam War

3. Quoted in Stanley Karnow, *Vietnam: A History*. New York: Penguin, 1997, pp. 197–98.
4. Quoted in *Time*, "The Fall of Dienbienphu," May 17, 1954. www .time.com.
5. Lyndon B. Johnson, "Radio and Television Report to the American People Following Renewed Aggression in the Gulf of Tonkin, August 4, 1964," American Presidency Project, 2017. www.presidency.ucsb.edu.
6. Quoted in Philip Caputo, *10,000 Days of Thunder: A History of the Vietnam War*. New York: Atheneum, 2005, p. 70.
7. Quoted in Karnow, *Vietnam*, p. 562.
8. Quoted in Robert Dallek, *Flawed Giant: Lyndon Johnson and His Times, 1961–1973*. New York: Oxford University Press, 1998, p. 509.

Chapter Two: How Did Fear of Communism Lead to US Intervention in Vietnam?

9. Quoted in Chalmers W. Roberts, "The Day We Didn't Go to War," *Reporter*, September 14, 1954. www.unz.org.
10. Quoted in Ted Morgan, *Valley of Death: The Tragedy at Dien Bien Phu That Led America into the Vietnam War*. New York: Random House, 2010, p. 408.
11. Karl Marx, *Critique of the Gotha Programme*, Marxists Internet Archive. www.marxists.org.
12. Dwight D. Eisenhower, "Letter from President Eisenhower to Ngo Dinh Diem, President of the Council of Ministers of Vietnam, October 23, 1954," Internet Modern History Sourcebook, Fordham University, 1998. http://sourcebooks.fordham.edu.

13. Quoted in Michael Kort, *The Columbia Guide to the Cold War*. New York: Columbia University Press, 1998, p. 24.
14. Quoted in Kort, *The Columbia Guide to the Cold War*, p. 28.
15. Quoted in David McCullough, *Truman*. New York: Simon & Schuster, p. 548.
16. Quoted in *Time*, "Foreign News: We Will Bury You," November 26, 1956. www.time.com.
17. Harry S. Truman, *The Autobiography of Harry S. Truman*. Boulder, CO: Associated University Press, 1980, p. 102.
18. Richard M. Nixon, "Meeting the People of Asia," *Department of State Bulletin*, January 4, 1954, p. 12.
19. Quoted in Wilbur H. Morrison, *The Tiger and the Elephant*. New York: Hippocrene, 1990, p. 14.
20. Quoted in Eisenhower National Historic Site, National Park Service, "The Quotable Quotes of Dwight D. Eisenhower." www.nps.gov.
21. Quoted in David L. Anderson, *The Columbia Guide to the Vietnam War*. New York: Columbia University Press, 2002, p. 50.

Chapter Three: How Did the Tet Offensive Increase Opposition to the War?

22. Quoted in James H. Willbanks, *The Tet Offensive: A Concise History*. New York: Columbia University Press, 2007, p. 21.
23. Quoted in Karnow, *Vietnam*, p. 527.
24. Quoted in Lewis Sorley, *Westmoreland: The General Who Lost Vietnam*. Boston: Houghton Mifflin Harcourt, 2011, p. 168.
25. Quoted in Kevin Robbie, "'Crack the Sky, Shake the Earth . . .': A Look Back at Tet," *Thursday Review*, February 14, 2015. www.thursdayreview.com.
26. Quoted in History, "Tet Offensive." www.history.com.
27. Allan Wendt, "Viet Cong Attack on Embassy Saigon, 1968," American Foreign Service Association, 2017. www.afsa.org.
28. Quoted in William Dudley and David Bender, eds., *The Vietnam War: Opposing Viewpoints*. San Diego, CA: Greenhaven, 1998, pp. 188–89.
29. Quoted in Clark Dougan and David Lipsman, *A Nation Divided*. Boston: Boston Publishing, 1984, p. 132.

30. Quoted in Sorley, *Westmoreland*, pp. 186, 187.

31. Quoted in Sorley, *Westmoreland*, p. 182.

32. Quoted in Douglas Brinkley, *Cronkite*. New York: HarperCollins, 2012, pp. 377–78.

33. David Halberstam, *The Powers That Be.* New York: Knopf, 1979, p. 514.

34. Quoted in Walter Cronkite, *A Reporter's Life.* New York: Knopf, 1996, p. 258.

35. Quoted in Don Oberdorfer, *Tet: The Turning Point in the Vietnam War.* Baltimore: Johns Hopkins University Press, 2001, p. 273.

36. Walter Cronkite, *The Vietnam War with Walter Cronkite: Tet!* CBS News, 1985. www.youtube.com/watch?v=T4qAYWBLYMs.

37. Quoted in Geoffrey Perret, *Commander in Chief: How Truman, Johnson, and Bush Turned a Presidential Power into a Threat to America's Future.* New York: Farrar, Straus & Giroux, 2007, p. 277.

38. James H. Willbanks, "Shock and Awe of Tet Offensive Shattered U.S. Illusions," *U.S. News & World Report*, January 29, 2009. www.usnews.com.

Chapter Four: How Did Richard Nixon's Policies Influence the War's Outcome?

39. Richard Nixon, "Address Accepting the Presidential Nomination at the Republican National Convention in Miami Beach, Florida, August 8, 1968," American Presidency Project, 2017. www.presidency.ucsb.edu.

40. Richard Nixon, *No More Vietnams.* New York: Arbor House, 1985, p. 106.

41. Quoted in Robert Young, "35,000 GIs to Leave Viet in 3 Months," *Chicago Tribune*, September, 17, 1969. www.chicagotribune.com.

42. Quoted in Robert Dallek, *Nixon and Kissinger: Partners in Power.* New York: HarperCollins, 2007, p. 118.

43. Quoted in Dallek, *Nixon and Kissinger*, p. 119.

44. Quoted in Robert D. Schulzinger, *A Time for War: The United States and Vietnam, 1941–1975.* New York: Oxford University Press, 1997, p. 289.

45. Richard Nixon, "Letters of the President and President Ho Chi Minh of the Democratic Republic of Vietnam, November 3, 1969," *American Presidency Project*, 2017. www.presidency.ucsb.edu.

46. Richard Nixon, "Address to the Nation on the War in Vietnam, November 3, 1969," *American Presidency Project*, 2017. www.presidency.ucsb.edu.

47. Quoted in Walter Isaacson, *Kissinger: A Biography.* New York: Simon & Schuster, 1992, pp. 163–64.

48. Quoted in Jeremi Suri, "The Nukes of October: Richard Nixon's Secret Plan to Bring Peace to Vietnam," *Wired*, February 25, 2008. www.wired.com.

49. Walter LaFeber, *The American Age: US Foreign Policy at Home and Abroad Since 1750.* New York: Norton, 1989, p. 613.

50. Quoted in Qiang Zhai, *China and the Vietnam Wars, 1950–1975.* Chapel Hill: University of North Carolina Press, 2000, p. 200.

51. Quoted in Walter Isaacson, *Kissinger*, p. 459.

52. Richard Nixon, "Address to the Nation Announcing Conclusion of an Agreement on Ending the War and Restoring Peace in Vietnam, January 27, 1973," *American Presidency Project*, 2017. www.presidency.ucsb.edu.

Chapter Five: What Lasting Impact Did the Vietnam War Have on the United States and Vietnam?

53. Robert S. McNamara, *In Retrospect: The Tragedy and Lessons of Vietnam.* New York: Times, 1995, p. 207.

54. Quoted in John Clark, "Vietnam Widows Share Their Pain," *Los Angeles Times*, January 24, 2000. www.latimes.com.

55. Quoted in Phil Coomes, "North Vietnamese Veterans Stories," *BBC News*, July 9, 2015. www.bbc.com.

56. George Black, "The Vietnam War Is Still Killing People," *New Yorker*, May 20, 2016. www.newyorker.com.

57. Quoted in Fred A. Wilcox, *Waiting for an Army to Die: The Tragedy of Agent Orange.* New York: Random House, 1983, p. 4.

58. Quoted in Agent Orange Record, "The Chemical Scythe," 2010. www.agentorangerecord.com.

59. Quoted in Jason Grotto and Tim Jones, "Agent Orange's Lethal Legacy: For U.S., a Record of Neglect," *Chicago Tribune*, December 4, 2009. www.chicagotribune.com.

60. Quoted in Don Wilkins, "Agent Orange Catching Up to Vietnam Veterans Decades Later," *Military Times*, February 27, 2016. www.miltarytimes.com.

61. Dan Rihn, "Vietnam: My Life After," This Is Viet Now. www.vietnow.com.

62. Quoted in Amy DePaul, "Trauma at Root of Mental Health Issues Among Vietnamese," Voice of OC, February 25, 2013. www.voiceofoc.org.

63. Jimmy Carter, "Our Nation's Past and Future," Jimmy Carter Presidential Library & Museum, 2016. www.jimmycarterlibrary.gov.

64. Quoted in Scott Laderman and Edwin A. Martini, eds., *Four Decades On: Vietnam, the United States, and the Legacies of the Second Indochina War*. Durham, NC: Duke University Press, 2013, p. 59.

65. Marvin Kalb, "It's Called the Vietnam Syndrome, and It's Back," Brookings Institution, January 22, 2013. www.brookings.edu.

Books

Christian G. Appy, *American Reckoning: The Vietnam War and Our National Identity*. New York: Penguin, 2015.

Alan Axelrod, *The Real History of the Vietnam War: A New Look at the Past*. New York: Sterling, 2013.

Clara Bingham, *Witness to the Revolution: Radicals, Resisters, Vets, Hippies, and the Year America Lost Its Mind and Found Its Soul*. New York: Random House, 2016.

Marvin Kalb and Deborah Kalb, *Haunting Legacy: Vietnam and the American Presidency from Ford to Obama*. Washington, DC: Brookings Institution, 2011.

Chris McNab, *50 Things You Should Know About the Vietnam War*. Lake Forest, CA: QEB, 2016.

Steve Sheinkin, *Most Dangerous: Daniel Ellsberg and the Secret History of the Vietnam War*. New York: Roaring Brook, 2015.

Internet Sources

Rick Campbell, "M-Day—1969: Millions Gather in the Name of Peace," *40 Years After* (blog), *Houston Chronicle*, November 19, 2009. http://blog.chron.com/40yearsafter/2009/11/m-day-1969-millions -gather-in-the-name-of-peace.

Time, "The Nation: Action in Tonkin Gulf," August 14, 1964. http:// content.time.com/time/subscriber/article/0,33009,897225,00.html.

Lynn Vavreck, "The Long Decline of Trust in Government, and Why That Can Be Patriotic," *New York Times*, July 3, 2015. www.nytimes .com/2015/07/04/upshot/the-long-decline-of-trust-in-government -and-why-that-can-be-patriotic.html.

Websites

American Experience: Vietnam Online (www.pbs.org/wgbh/amex /vietnam). This is the companion website to PBS's series on the Vietnam War. It contains a timeline, biographies of important people, and maps of Vietnam from 1945 to the postwar period.

Vietnam War, History (www.history.com/topics/vietnam-war). This comprehensive website features videos and information on weapons used in the war, antiwar protests, the presidents who led the United States in the war, and the war's important battles.

Vietnam War, History Place (www.historyplace.com/unitedstates /vietnam). This site presents an extremely detailed timeline of the Vietnam War from 1945 to 1975, including quotes and analysis of events.

Vietnam War Protests (www.history.com/topics/vietnam-war/viet nam-war-protests). This website examines the protest movement and includes several videos.

Virtual Exhibits on Communism (www.museumoncommunism.org). This is a comprehensive site that presents the philosophy, history, and atrocities of communism.